THE NEW
you

RANDY GILBERT

THE NEW YOU

**Discovering Your
True Nature in Christ**

Unless otherwise indicated, all Scripture quotations are taken from the *King James Version* of the Bible.

Scripture quotations marked NIV are taken from the *Holy Bible, New International Version®*. NIV®. Copyright © 1973, 1978, 1984 by International Bible Society. Used by permission of Zondervan Publishing House. All rights reserved.

Scripture quotations marked AMP are taken from *The Amplified Bible. Old Testament* copyright © 1965, 1987 by Zondervan Corporation, Grand Rapids, Michigan. *New Testament* copyright © 1958, 1987 by the Lockman Foundation, La Habra, California. Used by permission.

Scripture quotations marked ASV are taken from the *American Standard Version.* Copyright © 1901 by Thomas Nelson & Sons and copyright © 1929 by International Council of Religious Education.

THE NEW YOU
ISBN-13: 978-0-9642046-6-9
ISBN-10: 0-9642046-6-5

Copyright © 2006 by Randy Gilbert

Printed in the United States of America. All rights reserved under International Copyright Law. Contents and/or cover may not be reproduced in whole or in part in any form without the express written consent of the Publisher, except for brief quotations in critical reviews or articles.

Randy Gilbert
8491 Chamberlayne Road
Richmond, Virginia 23227

Contents

Introduction..1

Part I – Your New Identity

Chapter 1 – Your New Name 5
Chapter 2 – Your Deliverance................................29
Chapter 3 – Your Freedom 49
Chapter 4 – Your New Nature................................63
Chapter 5 – Your New Structure 79

Part II – Your New Life

Chapter 6 – Power for Life 95
Chapter 7 – The Power Walk 111
Chapter 8 – The Power Principle..........................129
Chapter 9 – The Power of Your Testimony 145
Chapter 10 – The Power Purge..............................161

Introduction

Do you remember the moment when you first gave your life to Jesus? I certainly do. After all these years, the memory is still fresh and clear. My circumstances were grim. Although I was a young man, I had been told that I was going to die from a terminal liver disease. I was at the end of my rope and desperate—I knew that only God could save me. As a result, I turned to Jesus and was born again and miraculously healed.

Despite the dramatic events that occurred that day, I did not fully grasp the magnitude of what God had done on the inside of me. Although I knew He had saved and healed me, what I didn't realize at the time was that an even greater miracle had occurred—my spiritual DNA had been changed forever. But God knew…and He began to lead me and guide me step by step, teaching me important truths about my new identity in Christ.

Learning to walk out your new identity as a Christian is a process, but regardless of what your circumstances might be right now, ***you are a new creature in Christ!*** The old you is gone, never to return. When you accepted Jesus, in that one defining moment you received a new beginning, a new identity, a new family, a new life—a whole new you!

As you read this book, it is my prayer that the Holy Ghost will open the eyes of your spirit and help you to take hold of the Truth and forever shake off the chains of your old sinful nature. One thing is certain—your life will never be the same.

—Pastor Randy Gilbert

PART I
YOUR NEW IDENTITY

"Him that overcometh will I make a pillar in the temple of my God, and he shall go no more out: and I will write upon him the name of my God, and the name of the city of my God, which is new Jerusalem, which cometh down out of heaven from my God: and I will write upon him my new name."

—Revelation 3:12

Chapter 1

Your New Name

Years ago, when I first gave my heart to Jesus and was born again, people kept telling me that I was a "new creature." *What in the world does that mean?* I wondered, *Am I not still Randy Gilbert?* But as I began to study the Word of God, it wasn't long before I began to find out what being a "new creature" meant. I discovered that everything I thought I knew or believed about myself had changed. As we explore the promises that the Word holds for all who trust in Jesus, you too will learn some things you didn't know before. You may be surprised by what you have been missing, and you will be challenged to redefine your identity. If you ever hope to reach your full potential and abundance of life in Christ, it's vitally important to know exactly who you are.

The Bible says, "Therefore, if anyone is in Christ, he is a new creation; the old has gone, the new has come! All this is from God, who reconciled us to himself through Christ and gave us the ministry of reconciliation: that God was reconciling the world to himself in Christ, not counting men's sins against them. And he has committed to us the message of reconciliation. We are therefore Christ's ambassadors, as though God were making his appeal through us. We implore you on Christ's behalf: Be reconciled to God. God made him who had no sin to be sin for us, so that in him we might become the righteousness of God" (2 Corinthians 5:17-21 NIV).

Experiencing the reality of these scriptures hinges on one condition: we must be *in Christ*. What exactly does it mean to be "in Christ"? Well, the Word clearly tells us that if we are to be in Christ, we must be born again. When you give your heart to Jesus, you have a new beginning that separates you from the world and your old sinful life. You are delivered out of the power of darkness and translated into a brand-new life in Christ.

This amazing truth is a wonderful mystery…a supernatural work of God that can only be received and understood by faith. But when Jesus encountered Nicodemus, He explained some of what being "born again" really means:

There was a man of the Pharisees, named Nicodemus, a ruler of the Jews: The same came to Jesus by night, and said unto him, Rabbi, we know that thou art a teacher come from God: for no man can do these miracles that thou doest, except God be with him. Jesus answered and said unto him, "Verily, verily, I say unto thee, Except a man be born again, he cannot see the kingdom of God." Nicodemus saith unto him, How can a man be born when he is old? can he enter the second time into his mother's womb, and be born? Jesus answered, "Verily, verily, I say unto thee, Except a man be born of water and of the Spirit, he cannot enter into the kingdom of God. That which is born of the flesh is flesh; and that which is born of the Spirit is spirit. Marvel not that I said unto thee, Ye must be born again. The wind bloweth where it listeth, and thou hearest the sound thereof, but canst not tell whence it cometh, and whither it goeth: so is every one that is born of the Spirit."

—John 3:1-8

Every person living on this planet is born of the flesh, having had a natural birth. But to be born again, or born from above, means that you are born of the Spirit. When you accept Christ, you experience a new *spiritual* birth. In that moment, you are baptized into His body. You become one with Him. You are in Him, and He is in you. Notice that 2 Corinthians 5:17 says, "If anyone *is* in Christ." It doesn't mention the future or the past. It doesn't say if any man *hopes* to be in Christ…or if you work long and hard enough, you'll finally be in Christ when you get to heaven. The word *is* means "now"—at this present time. **Now** you are a new creature. **Now** you are in Christ.

Perhaps you are thinking, *All right, I'm born again, therefore I am in Christ. But what does that* really *mean? How does that change anything?* First, to be in Christ means that you have been separated from the world by the blood of Jesus. When you were saved, you were delivered out of the power of darkness and translated into the kingdom of His dear Son. You are no longer a part of this world.

You may be thinking, *Wait a minute! My feet are still firmly planted on planet Earth. I still hear, see, and feel the things around me, and I'm pretty sure that I'm not in heaven yet!* That's all true. But in this case, the word "world" does not refer to the natural, physical planet. It refers to the part of creation that you belong to.

> WHEN YOU ACCEPTED JESUS, YOU WERE DELIVERED OUT OF THE OLD CREATION AND ITS SYSTEM.

You see, when you accepted Jesus, you were delivered out of the old creation and its system. You changed locations, even though you're on the same planet. You changed families. You are no longer a part of the family of Adam—you are now a part of the family of God. This means that all the sin and darkness in the world—everything destructive and damnable that resulted from Satan's actions and Adam's fall—are now broken off your life.

Jesus purchased a completely new life for each one of us. The simple fact that He defeated sin on the cross means that *right now* sin is defeated in our lives. We have been separated from it by the blood of Jesus. We have authority over sin and, consequently, through faith in the Word of God, we can now walk in that authority and literally tread on the enemy.

Unfortunately, this doesn't always mean that our natural circumstances suddenly change. New believers often become discouraged when they discover that they still have to deal with many of the same problems, temptations, and circumstances they experienced in their "old" lives. I remember being faced with these things. When I was first saved and started growing in the things of God, there seemed to be a lot of junk from my old life that was trying to follow me. It wasn't so much *what* I had done, as the *repercussions* of what I had done. The consequences of sin have a nasty way of cropping up when they aren't wanted.

But the Bible says, "Wherefore henceforth know we no man after the flesh: yea, though we have known Christ after the flesh, yet now henceforth know we him no more" (2 Corinthians 5:16). All of us were born of the flesh, but now that we are in Christ, we have to get our thinking straight. Jesus defeated sin on the cross. Now we must do our part by standing our ground and refusing to identify with our old flesh. We have to say and believe with our hearts, "Who I used to be is not who I am now."

The second half of this scripture addresses how we identify with Christ. "We have known Christ after the flesh…." This doesn't mean that Christ was sinful—rather, that He was born as a natural man. He was and is the Son of God, but He was also the Son of Man. It was necessary that Jesus be born as a flesh-and-blood man in order to pay the price for our sin. But He had to be all man *and* all God, because only a *sinless* man could redeem the children of Adam.

So the world knew Christ as a natural man (after the flesh), and for many unbelievers today, this is the extent of their understanding of Jesus. He was known in Nazareth as a child; on the shores of Galilee, He was known as the One who preached and laid healing hands on people; in Jerusalem, He was known as a teacher in the temple. People could touch Him. They walked and talked with Him. They ate dinner with Him.

What's wrong with all that? Nothing! But Jesus wasn't just a man who lived and died like any other.

He wasn't just a man who died a horrible death on a cross. He isn't just a famous historical figure. When we are *in Christ*, we don't know Him that way anymore. We know Him for who He is ***now***. He is raised from the dead! He is seated at the right hand of God. He still has a physical body, but it's a different body, a glorified body. Jesus is now the new man. Hallelujah!

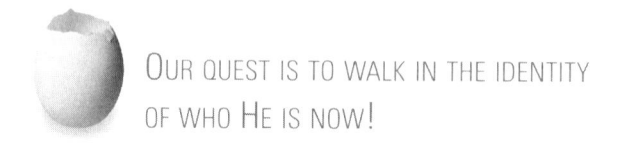

> OUR QUEST IS TO WALK IN THE IDENTITY OF WHO HE IS NOW!

In order to understand who we are in Christ, we must identify with who Jesus is, because as He is, so are we in this world. We can't just try to become like Jesus as He was on the shores of Galilee. Our quest is to walk in the identity of who He is now!

OUT WITH THE OLD, IN WITH THE NEW

Jesus is now the new man. But in order to understand the full significance of that, we must consider the identity and characteristics of the old man…Adam. The Bible says, "And God said, Let us make man in our image, after our likeness: and let them have dominion over the fish of the sea, and over the fowl of the air, and over the cattle, and over all the earth, and over every creeping thing that creepeth upon the earth. So God created man in his own image, in the image of God created he him; male and female created he them" (Genesis 1:26-27).

When we look at everything God has created—and He did purposefully create *everything*—we can see a commonality that runs through all of His creation. All things came out of Him. Just as with any artistic expression of human creativity, you can catch a glimpse of the Creator in the work of His hands. But this scripture very clearly tells us that Adam alone was created *in the image* of God, which means that Adam had characteristics and abilities like God. All other created things were in a completely different category. But Adam was set apart—above everything else in the natural realm.

Now, we know that every person on this planet has been born through a natural birth. This means we have all been born of Adam…into a physical body created in the image of God. God gave Adam certain traits and characteristics, and as Adam's descendants, each one of us shares those same traits. The Bible says, "The LORD God formed man of the dust of the ground, and breathed into his nostrils the breath of life; and man became a living soul" (Genesis 2:7). Adam came out of God. His spirit—that which gave him life—was literally blown into his lifeless body by God himself. And each of us is physically created after the same type…we too are created in the image of God.

That might have been the end of the story if Adam and Eve had not disobeyed God. But once they did, a new trait entered Adam's DNA—sin. And we have inherited that characteristic too. There's no getting around it…man is born with a sinful nature. Adam—the old man—had failed, and now God had to find a way to redeem His people. God needed a new man.

The Bible says, "And so it is written, The first man Adam was made a living soul; the last Adam was made a quickening spirit" (1 Corinthians 15:45). The "last Adam" is Jesus, and He has characteristics that are completely different from the first Adam. One big difference is that Adam was a created son, but Jesus, the last Adam, is a *born* son. You see, when Jesus was talking to Nicodemus, He was explaining to him that although everyone is born of a natural birth, there is another birth. He called it being born from above. We can be born of the Spirit of God, and that new birth is what makes a person a new man.

First Corinthians 15 goes on to say: "The first man is of the earth, earthy: the second man is the Lord from heaven. As is the earthy, such are they also that are earthy: and as is the heavenly, such are they also that are heavenly. And as we have borne the image of the earthy, we shall also bear the image of the heavenly" (vv. 47-49).

Do you see that—*the second man*? The second man, the second Adam—the last Adam, the new man. All these terms are synonymous. Jesus is the new man who was born of heaven, and if you are in Christ, you too are a new man and you bear His image! When Jesus died at Calvary and was raised from the dead, He established the new creation. That's why He is called the progenitor of our faith—He was the first one. And all the characteristics of the new creation are in the new man. So when you are born again, you get the new man, the new nature, the new type!

Perhaps you have some trouble accepting that your very nature—that which makes you who you are—could be so dramatically altered in a single moment. But this is what God's plan of redemption is all about.

When you can truly grasp the revelation of the fact that you are a new man, then your perspective of everything that happens around you is forever changed. You realize that this is who you are in Christ!

PART OF HIS BODY

The benefits of being a new man are limitless, but there are a few characteristics of your identity in Christ that are particularly important. First, the Bible says that God "hath raised us up together, and made us sit together in heavenly places in Christ Jesus" (Ephesians 2:6). Now, how can you and I be seated in heaven while we're standing on the earth? Well, first of all, we are *in Christ* and that's where He is seated, but the reality is that it is another dimension. That's part of the glory of the new creation. You have a quickening spirit now. That's how you can be in two places at once.

> IF WE ARE IN CHRIST, THEN EVERYTHING THAT GOD WILLED TO HIS SON, JESUS, IS NOW ALSO OURS.

Romans 8:17 also tells us that we are joint-heirs with Christ. In simple terms, this means that God has a "Last Will and Testament," and He has passed everything to His Son. Now, to be a joint heir means that your name is on the same line with Jesus' name. So you are an equal inheritor to the throne of God. Now, this means that if we are in Christ, then everything that God willed to His Son, Jesus, is now also ours. That is the basis of your inheritance. You are a joint heir with Christ.

We are also members of His natural body, bone of His bone and flesh of His flesh. The Bible says, "Now you are the body of Christ, and each one of you is a part of it" (1 Corinthians 12:27 NIV). That doesn't sound like some kind of distant association or relationship. You aren't a second-class citizen. If you are born again, you are an integral part of Christ himself.

Blessed be the God and Father of our Lord Jesus Christ, who hath blessed us with all spiritual blessings in heavenly places in Christ: according as he hath chosen us in him before the foundation of the world, that we should be holy and without blame before him in love: having predestinated us unto the adoption of children by Jesus Christ to himself, according to the good pleasure of his will, to the praise of the glory of his grace, wherein he hath made us accepted in the beloved. …Having made known unto us the mystery of his will, according to his good pleasure which he hath purposed in himself: that in the dispensation of the fullness of times he might gather together in one all things in Christ, both which are in heaven, and which are on earth; even in him: in whom also we have obtained an inheritance, being predestinated according to the purpose of him who worketh all things after the counsel of his own will.

—Ephesians 1:3-6,9-11

What a promise! You are accepted. You are beloved. God chose you before you were even born! Therefore, if you are seated in heavenly places in Christ Jesus; if you are a joint heir with Christ; if you are a member of Christ's body; if you are part of the covenant and He shares everything with you…doesn't it only stand to reason that He would also share His name?

The Bible tells us that it is so—that we bear His name, "…that worthy name by the which ye are called" (James 2:7). You have a new name! You are called by the name of Jesus. Hallelujah! Blessed be the name that is above every name.

> YOU HAVE A NEW NAME! YOU ARE CALLED BY THE NAME OF JESUS.

WALKING IN DOMINION

Receiving a revelation of your new name in Christ is the cornerstone that makes it possible for us to walk in dominion. *Webster's Dictionary* defines *dominion* as "domain," which means, "a sphere of knowledge, influence, or activity; a region distinctively marked by some physical feature; a territory over which dominion is exercised." Each of these definitions holds an important key to walking in victory as a new creation.

First, you have "a sphere of influence"—a perimeter that encompasses everything that you touch and everything that affects you in return. In other words, your life is your dominion. Because you are on Earth, everything that happens on this planet in the natural realm and the spiritual realm will affect you in some way. And that realm of influence filters down through your country, your state, your neighborhood, and your own home. It extends to your family and friends, your job, personal acquaintances, fellow believers, and even strangers you encounter on the street. Wherever you go, whatever you encounter, or whoever is touched by your existence lies within your dominion.

We know that the blood of Jesus separated your life from the world when you became born again. Your life was purchased by the blood of Jesus, and now you belong to Him. As a result, there is literally a bloodline that goes all the way around you, sanctifying or separating you from the old creation. That bloodline is the physical feature that marks your territory and clearly defines your dominion. Everything that was a part of the old man—the old nature, the old creation—now lies outside that boundary, and it can't cross over the line unless you allow it.

When you were born again, you gave your life to Jesus. But He gave it back to you and said "I want you to rule and reign in your life with My authority." It is imperative that we bear His name, because the name of Jesus gives us the authority and power to walk in victory. His Word tells us that when He washed you in His blood, gave you His Word, and gave you His name, Jesus fully equipped you to exercise dominion and conquer the enemy in your own life.

The key is that we must *exercise* dominion. You can't be passive because of ignorance, disbelief, or apathy and expect to have victory. If you walk according to the old man, denying who you are in Christ, you won't have dominion. There is no victory for the old man. This is why so many believers are still bound today and why so many within the church are not receiving the promises of God in their lives.

Receiving and acting on the knowledge of who you are in Christ is literally how you walk in victory as a believer. Walking in the authority of your new name is how you exercise dominion over the forces of darkness. That's how you kick sin out of your life. That's how you kick sickness out of your life. That's how you kick poverty out of your life. That's how you kick strife out of your life. That's how you kick out every curse and negative effect of the world. It's how you get over whatever has happened to you in the past. When you know who you are in Christ and you stand in the authority of your new name and exercise your dominion, then you will walk in the victory that Jesus died to give you.

Are there areas in your own life where you are not walking in victory? Are you getting run over by the forces of darkness? Are you being held captive in some area of your life? Are there unresolved issues with sin, your job, or your family? Are you suffering from sickness in your body? Are you struggling financially? If so, you have been invaded by the enemy. Your perimeter has been breached.

> IF YOU ARE TIRED OF THE DEVIL TRESPASSING INTO YOUR AREAS OF DOMINION, DRIVE HIM OUT.

If you are tired of the devil trespassing into your areas of dominion, the only solution is to drive him out. If you are ready to use the authority that you have in the name of Jesus and banish the enemy from your life, than pray the following prayer out loud:

Lord Jesus, I believe in my heart that You are raised from the dead. I confess with my mouth that You are Lord. Therefore, I am saved. I am a new creature. You are my Savior, Lord Jesus, and I am delivered. Lord Jesus, I am washed in Your blood.

My life, everything about me, is now protected by Your blood. Lord Jesus, Your blood is literally the line that separates me and everything within my dominion from the powers of darkness. Your precious blood is my line of defense.

Lord Jesus, the Word declares that You have given me Your own name. I choose to exercise my dominion by the authority of the name that is above all names. As a joint heir with Christ, I have the name and I use the name right now. So in the name of Jesus, I take dominion over every work of the enemy in my life. No evil thing has the right to touch me. I command all sin, all of the servants of the enemy, all the works of darkness, and all the consequences of the old world to get out!

Thank You, Lord Jesus, that within this bloodline You have placed around my life, only Your promises prevail. Remind me by the Holy Spirit to be diligent and faithful to exercise dominion in my life with Your name and by the power of Your Word. By faith I declare that Your promises are all that I will receive into my life. In the name of Jesus, I am delivered. Hallelujah!

Can you see that bloodline? By faith, can you see it guarding every aspect of your life, every corner of your territory? It is all around your property and possessions, your family, your children, your job, your finances, your health, and your future. The devil is defeated—for you have been given His name and therefore walk in dominion. Praise the Lord!

STUDY GUIDE

Losing your identity can be a scary thing. It often feels as though your equilibrium has suddenly shifted in such a way that it is sometimes hard to get your balance! When you accept Christ, you are suddenly different—your old man is no more, even though you still have to deal with the consequences of the old man's choices. Take a moment to consider where you were then and where you are now. You should have much to rejoice about, and a good idea of the areas that still need to be changed into His likeness.

1. What was your life like before you accepted Christ? What memories, thoughts, or impressions do you recall from your salvation experience? How did you *know* that you had an encounter with God? What evidence was there—in your natural or inner self—that you were forever changed?

2. How would you describe Jesus to someone who doesn't know who He is? Do you envision Him hanging on the cross and dying for your sins? Why does it matter that He was raised from the dead? How does His resurrection affect your life here and now?

3. Natural circumstances don't always change overnight, even though you have a new spirit in Christ. What problems did you continue to struggle with after you were saved? Are you still challenged by the temptations and nature of your old man? What characteristics of that old man are now completely changed?

…The term revolution…has a special meaning.…It is not a question of the Old Man transforming himself into the New, but of the New Man becoming alive to the fact that he is new, that he has been transformed already without his having realized it.

—W. H. Auden

Chapter 2

Your Deliverance

You now know that once you are in Christ, you are a new man (or woman). But what happens to the old man? To put it simply: the old man is dead. If you are a Christian, then the old you is gone. Glory to God!

The Bible encourages us to "put off concerning the former conversation the old man, which is corrupt according to the deceitful lusts; and be renewed in the spirit of your mind; and that ye put on the new man, which after God is created in righteousness and true holiness" (Ephesians 4:22-24).

This passage of Scripture is talking about behavior—how we can demonstrate in the natural what God has already done for us in the Spirit. According to our declaration of faith in Christ, the old man is dead, but we must also take action so that our new man can rise up in newness of life to rule and reign. Christ rules *in* you and *through* you, so that your spirit can take dominion over that outer man—your flesh—and bring him into subjection. You need to cast aside the old man, and "put on" the new man—not out of arrogance or pride or with a religious spirit, but in obedience and faith that what God has said is true. Now, that is really what the Christian lifestyle is all about—realizing who you are and then acting according to that identity.

As we study the Word of God in order to learn how to bring the outer man into subjection, the term "flesh" can be confusing at times. The word is used frequently in both a negative and positive sense. It appears often in the New Testament to denote both the temporal—the earthly and physical characteristics of man—as well as the debased nature of unregenerate man. So when we come across this term, it is necessary to pay close attention to the context of the scripture to determine how it is being used.

The apostle Paul wrote to the Corinthians concerning the temporal flesh: "For though we walk in the flesh, we do not war after the flesh: (For the weapons of our warfare are not carnal, but mighty through God to the pulling down of strong holds)" (2 Corinthians 10:3-4). This passage of Scripture could really be translated to say, "Though we walk in the *natural* (a physical body), we do not war after the natural (the physical). Our warfare is spiritual in nature. We are not fighting against flesh and blood, but against spiritual darkness."

In Galatians 5:19-21, we see the word "flesh" used again in a very different way: "Now the works of the flesh are manifest, which are these; Adultery, fornication, uncleanness, lasciviousness, idolatry, witchcraft, hatred, variance, emulations, wrath, strife, seditions, heresies, envyings, murders, drunkenness, revellings, and such like: of the which I tell you before, as I have also told you in time past, that they which do such things shall not inherit the kingdom of God." In this context, it is obvious that this refers to the "flesh" in its most negative connotation: the sinful nature of unregenerate man, which has no place in the new creation.

ONCE WE ARE IN CHRIST, WE RECEIVE A COMPLETELY NEW NATURE.

As Christians, you and I must understand that we no longer need to worry about those "fleshly" manifestations. Once we are in Christ, we receive a completely new nature. Now, it is true that your physical body is born of the corruptible type of Adam, and your body and carnal mind have a proclivity towards darkness—but that's not a nature. Your body will go where you direct it. If you leave it ungoverned, it will go back towards darkness, but your true nature comes out of your spirit. You don't have two natures within you. There is only one you, and if you are born again, the real you is born after Christ! You have a righteous nature!

Perhaps you are thinking, *Well, I don't understand why I still struggle.* Why do we still have battles? It's a matter of whether you are strong enough spiritually to rise up and take dominion over the outer man. The outer man does not have his own nature. The outer man is a follower—at least he's supposed to be. Your body is really nothing but a tool to be used while you're here on Earth. But one day, in the twinkling of an eye—

whether in the resurrection or the rapture—your body will be changed. The corruption in your body, which is the signature of death, will be burned out. Then you will be physically resurrected in the likeness of Christ.

Carnal Christianity

By definition, for Christians to "walk in the flesh" is to conduct their lives as though they are not born again. That is the reason we need to put off the old man. Now, he's dead already, but we just don't want to act like him. The very reason we are able to do that is because he is dead, and we have new life within us. We can choose to walk in the life of Christ.

Many times people will use the phrase "a carnal Christian." What does that mean? Well, it's essentially talking about a person who is born again but isn't acting like it. The apostle Paul, speaking to the Corinthian church, gives us a clear definition of this type of carnality: "And I, brethren, could not speak unto you as unto spiritual, but as unto carnal, even as unto babes in Christ" (1 Corinthians 3:1). Notice the correlation between being immature babes and being carnal, as opposed to being spiritual. True spirituality, by biblical definition, comes through maturity.

Paul goes on to say, "I have fed you with milk, and not with meat: for hitherto ye were not able to bear it, neither yet now are ye able" (v. 2). There is another passage in the book of Hebrews that points out very clearly that meat belongs to mature believers and milk belongs to the babes. If we want to grow in Christ, at some point we have to decide, "Okay, I'm not satisfied with just milk anymore; now I'm going to find some meat." And the meat of God's Word is what makes us strong and causes us to develop maturity.

Still addressing the Christians of Corinth, Paul says, "For ye are yet carnal: for whereas there is among you envying, and strife, and divisions, are ye not carnal, and walk as men? For while one saith, I am of Paul; and another, I am of Apollos; are ye not carnal?" (1 Corinthians 3:3-4). You see, a carnal Christian still walks in the nature of the old man. Here, by definition, carnality involves envy, strife, and division.

How many born-again believers walk in envy, strife, and division? Sadly, it is rampant in the church today. Here Paul specifically addresses one common cause of division within the church. When he says "while one saith, I am of Paul; and another, I am of Apollos," he is really talking about how some people have a tendency to gravitate toward one leader, while others follow someone else. Eventually, this results in the formation of multiple camps, with believers—who are all part of the same body of Christ—becoming set against each other on the basis of differing doctrines and teachings. Suspicion and distrust set in…all because we sound a little different, or act a little differently.

You see, the divisions that man has erected within the church are because of spiritual weakness and immaturity. And nothing makes the enemy happier than when different parts of the body of Christ can't get along. But spiritual maturity says, "Now wait a minute, this brother or sister is washed in the blood of the Lamb and is born of the same Spirit. I can see past those inconsequential differences and see the Christ-man in him or her, who is just like me."

Many divisions in the body of Christ are based on natural things. Carnal Christians prefer to be identified by what they perceive to be the most important distinction or quality about themselves. Gender, race, economic status, family origins, education, profession—all can hinder unity within the body of Christ. But as you get stronger in the Lord, you don't need to have a distinction that sets you apart. It's enough to be identified with Him. You don't need to be separated from your brethren—you need to be separated from the world. If you want a distinction to grab hold of, that's the one that you need. You are a Christian and you're separated from the world.

> YOU ARE SOMEBODY IN CHRIST. YOU DON'T NEED AN OLD-MAN CRUTCH.

You see, in Christ, none of those things exist, because it all involves the outer man. The Adamic man, or the old man, is always looking for a way to be separate from God. All of that is nothing more than a crutch, a way to feel like "somebody." But you need to understand that you are somebody *in Christ*. You don't need an old-man crutch. You don't need a worldly identity to have dignity and strength. You need to identify with who you are in Christ. The name of Jesus is above every name, and you are called by that name. How can it possibly get any better than that? What more could you possibly want?

Think On These Things

Now, as we grow spiritually in Christ, our new inner man rises up and is able to take dominion over the outer man—even over our own thoughts. Taking dominion over how we think is critical if we want to put an end to the old man and his carnal ways. Just because you *think* something is right, or because you were taught that way, or because everyone you know believes it, does not make it true. The Bible says, "We demolish arguments and every pretension that sets itself up against the knowledge of God, and we take captive every thought to make it obedient to Christ" (2 Corinthians 10:5 NIV). This means that every time a thought, idea, or temptation that does not line up with the Word of God comes across our minds, we have to say to ourselves (sometimes out loud) "That's not right! That's not Christlike! I'm not going to think that way any more. I take that thought captive in the name of Jesus and cast it down!"

Remember, we read earlier that to put on the new man you must be "renewed in the spirit of your mind" (Ephesians 4:23). Why is this so important? Because for our entire lives, the world has been influencing us. Until we become born again and receive a new life in the Spirit, we are wholly a part of the world and its system. We have old-man thoughts and old-man ideas, and we are likely to believe most of what all the other "old men" out in the world proclaim to be truth. What comes naturally to us in our way of thinking is of the old nature, not the new man and the nature of Christ. And often we make decisions and take action in our lives based on what we think—not necessarily what is right in the kingdom of God or what the nature of our new man would dictate. This is why Paul wrote, "Do not conform any longer to the pattern of this world, but be transformed by the renewing of your mind. Then you will be able to test and approve what God's will is—his good, pleasing and perfect will" (Romans 12:2 NIV).

We must separate ourselves from the behavior and thoughts of the old man. If we don't, the consequences are severe. The Bible makes this clear: "For to be carnally minded is death; but to be spiritually minded is life and peace" (Romans 8:6). To continue thinking according to the carnal nature results in spiritual death. This is why so many Christians are walking around right now sick in their bodies, bound by poverty and lack, controlled by addiction, and not fulfilling the call of

God on their lives. But to be spiritually minded allows us to discern God's good and perfect will. It results in spiritual life and peace. It makes it possible for our new man to take dominion and for the blessings of the new creation to flow in our lives.

How do we know what is right and what to think? First, we must study the Word of God and ask the Holy Spirit to illuminate the Scriptures to change the way we think. Many people in the world believe they have an understanding or knowledge of the Bible, but in reality the old man can't grasp the truth. Once we become born again, however, the new man—the new nature of Christ that now lives within us—recognizes and responds to the life contained within God's Word. The Bible even gives us a guideline by which to judge our thoughts: "Finally, brethren, whatsoever things are true, whatsoever things are honest, whatsoever things are just, whatsoever things are pure, whatsoever things are lovely, whatsoever things are of good report; if there be any virtue, and if there be any praise, think on these things. Those things, which ye have both learned, and received, and heard, and seen in me, do: and the God of peace shall be with you" (Philippians 4:8-9). Now that is truth to live by!

The Blood of Jesus

When you accept who you are in Christ, you are accepting your true deliverance. You see, it's not just the devil that you need to get set free from—it is sin. That is the real culprit, because the devil would never have any real control over your life if it weren't for sin.

The enemy loves to come after you and condemn you for the things that you have done. He loves trying to convince you that there's no way out. If he succeeds, condemnation makes you feel like you're stuck. But when Jesus deals with you, He always shows you the way out. You may need to repent, but He never leaves you in a corner. He never puts you down. He never condemns you. "There is therefore now no condemnation to them which are in Christ Jesus, who walk not after the flesh, but after the Spirit" (Romans 8:1). The Lord is good!

By the power of the blood of Jesus, the power of sin is broken and that eliminates the devil's control. He no longer has any place in you when you're washed in the blood of the Lamb. An important theological term that applies here is *efficacy*—the efficacy of the blood. This means that the blood of Jesus is effective for its purpose beyond description. The blood cannot

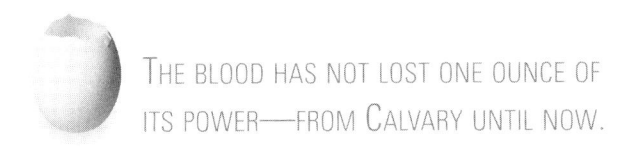

> THE BLOOD HAS NOT LOST ONE OUNCE OF ITS POWER—FROM CALVARY UNTIL NOW.

be replaced by anything else, and it cannot be changed, altered, or tampered with by mankind. Isn't that good news? That is why when a person confesses Christ, the blood is applied to them afresh and anew, and their sins are washed away, as though they had never been committed in the first place. The blood is just as effective today as it was on the day that Jesus' disciples believed on Him right after He was raised from the dead. The blood has not lost one ounce of its power—from Calvary until now. Hallelujah!

Now, you have to honestly and sincerely believe the Word of God. You have to hold the things of God in trust and honor in your life. You can't play around. The holiness of the blood of Jesus goes beyond human description, so you can't hold these things in contempt. But they belong to you. You have a right to touch the holy things of God, and the blood of Jesus is always there for you. So no matter what situation you may find yourself in, you can always turn to Jesus.

Your identification with Christ and knowing who you are in Him enable you to look temptation in the face and say, "This time I'm not falling for it. I'm not going to go for it, in Jesus' name. I have already been delivered. Glory to God!" And when you realize who you are and build up that inner man in Christ, then you are able to exercise dominion—over yourself, then over your own mind, and finally over your life.

THE OLD MAN IS DEAD

The Bible says, "Know ye not, that so many of us as were baptized into Jesus Christ were baptized into his death? Therefore we are buried with him by baptism into death: that like as Christ was raised up from the dead by the glory of the Father, even so we also should walk in newness of life" (Romans 6:3-4).

First, it's important to understand that water baptism is a reflection or physical demonstration of salvation. When you were born again, you were baptized into the body of Christ. So according to this scripture, when you were baptized into—or saved by—Jesus Christ, you were also baptized into His death. Now, there is an important parallel here. Jesus died physically, but then He was raised up. He's now the new man, and He walks in the newness of life. In the same way, when you accept Jesus, your old man is put to death, and you are raised up again in new life in Christ.

The apostle Paul goes on to say, "For if we have been planted together in the likeness of his death, we shall be also in the likeness of his resurrection: knowing this, that our old man is crucified with him, that the body of sin might be destroyed, that henceforth we should not serve sin. For he that is dead is freed from sin" (vv. 5-7). The new birth is the resurrection for you. So, like Christ, you are now walking in the newness of life, and the old man is dead.

> IF YOU ARE LOOKING FOR THE JESUS THAT IS HANGING ON THE CROSS, YOU WON'T FIND HIM.

Many people treasure the crucifix—a cross that depicts Jesus hanging there in the agony of His death. Truly, the price that Christ paid for us was incomprehensible and should not be taken lightly or forgotten. But I have news for you—if you are looking for the Jesus that is hanging on the cross, you won't find Him. He no longer exists! Jesus will never be that way again.

He is not coming back to earth in that original form to live and die again for anybody. Jesus is now the new man—resurrected and forever changed.

When you accepted Jesus as your Savior, what happened to Christ is the same thing that has happened to you. That old man was nailed to the cross. You put the old man to death, and the process of salvation resurrected you in the likeness of Christ. That's who you are now, and you can't go back. You couldn't go back if you wanted to. You've been delivered from the world and raised up in the newness of life. You are a new creature in Christ.

Study Guide

Do you ever wonder why Christians seem to have the most problems…and can be the most difficult people to get along with? Envy, strife, division, pride, addiction, and many more sins of the flesh are rampant in the church, which means that many, many believers are practicing "carnal Christianity." The old man is dead, and the new man is alive in Christ. It's time we started acting like it!

1. God has given you a brand-new spirit. How should that reality manifest in your everyday life? What can you do to begin changing how you act? What areas do you struggle with most in your life?

2. What does it mean to "renew the spirit of your mind"? (See Ephesians 4:23.) What is the nature of your "self talk"? When you are challenged by thoughts that are not of God, do you speak the Word, or do you imitate the common attitudes and speech of the world? What are some examples of thoughts that come to your mind—or sometimes come out of your mouth—that don't line up with the Word of God? What does the Bible say about the battle of the mind and the importance of our thought lives? (See Proverbs 23:7; 2 Corinthians 10:5; Philippians 4:8.)

"Take my yoke upon you, and learn of me; for I am meek and lowly in heart: and ye shall find rest unto your souls. For my yoke is easy, and my burden is light."

—Matthew 11:29-30

You have freedom when you're easy in your harness.

—Robert Frost

Chapter 3

Your Freedom

Let's look again at 2 Corinthians 5:21: "For he hath made him to be sin for us, who knew no sin; that we might be made the righteousness of God in him." Notice that it does not say that we might *hope* to be righteous—it says we are *made* righteous in Christ. By definition, *righteousness* means "right standing" or "to be right" with God. Jesus said, "I am the way, the truth, and the life: no man cometh unto the Father, but by me" (John 14:6). This means there is no other way to be in God's presence—to "be right" with Him—except through faith in Christ. When you accept Jesus, you receive His salvation as a free gift. In that moment, His righteousness is also given to you and you are *made* righteous. You simply can't have it without Jesus. It doesn't have anything to do with your behavior—it is a miraculous work of faith and grace.

Now, religion tries to use external controls—rules, regulations, and the traditions of men—to change people's behavior so they can "act" righteous. But God starts with the inner man—He changes your spirit and then works His way outward. So, in order to walk in victory, you have to acknowledge every good thing that is within you in Christ Jesus. You have to confess, "I have been made righteous," instead of thinking, *Do I feel righteous?* Or *do I act righteous?* That's irrelevant. The fruit of righteousness will come later. What matters most is that your nature has been changed and you have been made right with God. Regardless of how you may feel or what struggles you may have in your life, your spirit is now made new through the righteousness of Christ.

How can your spirit have a nature that is separate from your outer man? Truthfully, the very existence of the spirit man is a mystery to many people. In fact,

> ALTHOUGH YOU MAY NOT BE AWARE OF YOUR SPIRIT, THE SPIRIT MAN IS WHO YOU REALLY ARE.

few people are even aware that they have a spirit before they become born again. But the Bible tells us that God created man as a triune being—meaning that man is a spirit, he has a soul, and he lives in a physical body. The Bible also says that God himself is a Spirit, and we were created in His image. So, although you may not be aware of your spirit, the spirit man is who you really are.

BODY, SOUL, AND SPIRIT

The trouble is that we often struggle with accepting something that we can't see and touch or that doesn't provide sufficient "proof" of its existence. When you look in the mirror, you can't see your spirit. Your body, on the other hand, is pretty obvious. You see it every day and respond to its need for nourishment, rest, and activity…and nothing is more tangible and "real" than when your body doesn't feel right. Pain and sickness have a considerable ability to make you very aware of the existence of your physical body!

While the body makes up our physical form, the soul consists of the mind, will, and emotions. Our thoughts and intellect, and the characteristics that make up our unique "personality" are predominant parts of our everyday lives. In fact, most people think that they actually are a body, and then relate to themselves predominantly through their personality.

But the existence, nature, and character of your spirit man are things that you have to accept by faith. You have to learn about your spirit through the Word of God, because although you can't see it and you can't feel it, it's still there. We have to "re-educate" ourselves in order to gain an understanding of this most critical part of our being.

You would have an equally difficult time relating to heaven if you had not been hearing about it all your life. In the western world, the concept of heaven has been popularized and secularized to the point that even people who don't believe in Jesus claim to believe in heaven. Most likely, you've been hearing about heaven ever since you were a child, and as a result you have a reference point for it and you can accept it. Well, the truth about who you are spiritually is the same. It's something that you can't see, yet it is more of a reality than what you do see.

A New Spirit

Unfortunately, what the Word of God has to say about our true identity in the Spirit has not been taught often enough in the church. As a result, many believers don't know how to relate to who they are in Christ, and they constantly struggle. Without a real understanding about our new identity, we will not be able to walk in the things of God. We must lay the foundation through faith, for it is central to living a victorious Christian life.

The Bible says, "A new heart will I give you and a new spirit will I put within you, and I will take away the stony heart out of your flesh and give you a heart of flesh. And I will put my Spirit within you and cause you to walk in My statutes, and you shall heed My ordinances and do them" (Ezekiel 36:26-27 AMP). God is saying, "I'm going to take out that old spirit, and I'm going to put in a new spirit. It's not just a cleaned-up old you. It's a brand-new you."

As a result of receiving a new heart of flesh, we begin to develop a passion for the things of God and a desire to please Him. That's what living the Christian life is all about. We are supposed to mature spiritually until, ultimately, our inner spirit man grows stronger and stronger and takes dominion over the outer man. You see, we were designed so that our spirit would be in charge. That's when things start to change in our lives, and we can overcome the struggle with sin and temptation. As we grow in the spirit and relate to God—spirit to Spirit—we begin to walk in freedom and victory.

MORE THAN CONQUERORS

What are some of the characteristics of this new spirit—your new nature? The Bible tells us, "And we know that in all things God works for the good of those who love him, who have been called according to his purpose. For those God foreknew he also predestined to be conformed to the likeness of his Son, that he might be the firstborn among many brothers. And those he predestined, he also called; those he called, he also justified; those he justified, he also glorified. ...In

> WE HAVE A NEW SPIRITUAL DNA THAT IS PROGRAMMED FOR VICTORY AND SUCCESS.

all these things we are more than conquerors through him who loved us" (Romans 8:28-30, 37 NIV). We are *more* than conquerors! We have a new spiritual DNA that is programmed for victory and success.

Romans 8:9 says, "But ye are not in the flesh, but in the Spirit, if so be that the Spirit of God dwell in you. Now if any man have not the Spirit of Christ, he is none of his." Now, this verse is saying that if you deny that you have an overcoming spirit, then you're really denying that you are born again. Because if you are in Christ, you are an overcomer. You can't have the Spirit of God dwelling in you and still have a spirit that fails. It isn't possible.

But I don't feel like an overcomer, you may be thinking. Or perhaps the circumstances in your life aren't all that victorious right now. But that is nothing more than the condition of your soul—which is the mind, the will, and the emotions—and your physical nature, or body, in the natural realm. Romans 8:11 says that the same Spirit that raised Jesus from the dead is in you. If you are born of the spirit of Christ, the *real* you is a born conqueror.

AN INCORRUPTIBLE SEED

Concerning the relationship between himself and the Father, Jesus said, "Anyone who has seen me has seen the Father" (John 14:9 NIV). The Bible also says that Jesus is the "express image" of the Father. (See Hebrews 1:3.) In the same way, if you are born of Christ, you have the same spirit—you are the spitting image of Him! Now, the really amazing thing is that even after you become born again, you are still you. You still have your unique personality and identity. You still have your name, but your spirit is no longer of Adam—your spirit is of God. You are in Him. You are still you—only better!

First Peter 1:23 says that we are "…born again, not of corruptible seed, but of incorruptible, by the word of God, which liveth and abideth for ever." Notice that we are born by the Word, which is an *incorruptible* seed. What exactly does that mean? To put it simply, there is no genealogical baggage. In the world today, we hear things all the time about how people have a "predisposition" to cancer, or chemical and substance abuse, or a tendency toward violence and other destructive behaviors. All these things—and more—are evidence of the corrupt nature passed down from Adam throughout all mankind. Because of his sin, Adam's seed was corruptible, and reproduced itself generation after generation. The result is that each one of us, in one form or another, were born into the natural world under generational curses—those sins and behavior patterns that were passed down from our ancestors, from parent to child, over and over again.

The good news is that according to the Scripture, we are now born of an incorruptible seed—after the genealogy of Jesus, who is sinless and perfect. That means that you are no longer inherently affected or controlled by generational curses. They no longer have any power to cause sickness, poverty, abuse, addiction, death, mental illness, or any other kind of destruction in your life. They can't hinder your destiny or keep you from receiving all the blessings of God's kingdom.

You're now in the family of God, and your only relatives are God the Father, God the Son, and God the Holy Ghost. You received all of Him: all of His nature, all of His power, all of His righteousness, all of His holiness—all of His characteristics in your new man. When you were born again, you received the whole package.

Now, if you don't have this revelation and you are struggling, trying to live the Christian life while keeping your old man alive, how do you respond to something like this? Well, all you can do is accept it. It's a free gift. This is what being a Christian is all about. This is why Jesus went to the cross—to change you.

> YOU HAVE BEEN MADE RIGHTEOUS BY THE SHED BLOOD OF JESUS CHRIST, AND YOU ARE MORE THAN A CONQUEROR!

The way you act and the way you see yourself in the mirror is not the real you. You are a new creature in Christ—old things are passed away, and all things have become new. You have been made righteous by the shed blood of the Lord Jesus Christ, and you are more than a conqueror! Greater is He that is in you than he that is in the world. You have total dominion, total victory in every area of your life. Hallelujah! This is the real you. This is your freedom.

Study Guide

Webster's Dictionary defines *freedom* as, "Liberation from slavery or restraint or from the power of another." Whether you realize it or not, you were born into bondage—you were a slave to sin and under the control of the kingdom of darkness. But Christ has paid your ransom, and through Him, you are redeemed from the enemy. No more do you have to be controlled or affected by the power of sin. No more are you held hostage by the enemy of your soul—you are free to walk in relationship with God.

1. Is there a difference between the "religion" of Christianity and relationship with Jesus Christ? How does true Christianity differ from the world's religious systems? Do rules and regulations that govern your actions have any redeeming qualities? How can focusing on external behavior lead to more bondage? How does Jesus want you to follow Him? (See Matthew 11:28-30.)

2. Have you struggled with specific issues and temptations in your life? Do others in your family have some of the same struggles? How have generational curses influenced your life? Is there a pattern that you can identify of sins and behavior patterns being passed down through your family? In what areas in your life has the power of God set you free?

But ye are a chosen generation, a royal priesthood, an holy nation, a peculiar people; that ye should show forth the praises of him who hath called you out of darkness into his marvelous light.

—1 Peter 2:9

The old man is dead now.

—Charles Phillips

Chapter 4

Your New Nature

In order to walk in our new identity, we have to renew our minds and shift our old way of thinking to line up with the Word of God. We've come to understand that when we are born again, then we are in Christ and receive a new nature, born of His Spirit. But what exactly does the Bible say about who we are? What are the important distinguishing traits of our new nature?

We are going to uncover some of the most important characteristics of the new nature, so that when the enemy comes after you with accusations, condemnation, and destruction—which he will—you will be prepared. When you know exactly who you are in Christ, you have the necessary ammunition to combat the attacks of the enemy and win the victory.

You Are Righteous

Now, the whole idea of walking in the new man, or walking in the spirit, is to live our daily lives in open communication with the Lord Jesus Christ, God the Father, and the Holy Spirit. The Bible tells us that before the fall, Adam communed with God—they would literally walk together in the garden during the cool of the day. Ever since, God has been seeking a way to restore that relationship with man, and now, through the free gift of righteousness in Christ, we are able to be in His presence and commune with Him again.

Righteous people sound a certain way before God. The Bible says that "the righteous are bold as a lion" (Proverbs 28:1). The righteous are not always making excuses. The righteous don't feel unworthy or low. And righteous people stand their ground in confidence. Think for a minute about the example of a lion—by their very nature or instinct, lions don't back up. When they encounter an enemy, they stand ready to fight. They show no fear, weakness, or timidity.

> OUR NEW MAN HAS BEEN GIVEN A CONFIDENT NATURE THAT DOESN'T BACK DOWN FROM THE ENEMY.

One time while visiting Africa, I witnessed a lion encounter a bull elephant. Despite the fact that the elephant was huge and a potential threat, that lion didn't back down. He didn't turn tail and run. He wasn't afraid of the challenge because boldness was ingrained in his genetic makeup. In the same way, our new nature carries with it an inherent boldness—not based on ourselves but on who we are in Christ. We know that we are loved and accepted by God and that we are worthy to have relationship with Him. And our new man has been given a confident nature that doesn't back down from the enemy.

YOU ARE HOLY

By definition, *holy* means, "pure," or having nothing in itself but one thing. Something that is holy is set apart and is one hundred percent pure—only controlled by one influence. God is holy. There's nothing in God but God. He doesn't have any other outside influences. So when He says that we are holy, He is saying that there is nothing within us but himself. Remember, our new nature is born of an incorruptible seed. In this new nature, there is nothing but Him. It's not mixed with another seed—it is a holy seed and, therefore, He has made you holy by nature.

Perhaps you are thinking, *I am definitely not holy! I can't get through the day without messing up. I try my best, but I just can't seem to cut it.* We're not talking about the way you act—we're talking about who you *are*. You see, once you recognize who you are and grow in that knowledge, your actions will start to line up with your nature. The Bible says "Blessed and holy is he that hath part in the first resurrection: on such the second death hath no power, but they shall be priests of God and of Christ, and shall reign with him a thousand years," (Revelation 20:6). Regardless of how you may feel and how you may struggle, according to the Word of God, you *are* holy. Hallelujah!

You Are Sanctified

First Corinthians 1:2 says, "Unto the church of God which is at Corinth, to them that are sanctified in Christ Jesus, called to be saints, with all that in every place call upon the name of Jesus Christ our Lord…." Did you notice that this verse says, "*are* sanctified," not "*trying to become sanctified*"? Now, if you study the Word, you'll discover that the book of Corinthians has more correction in it than any of the other New Testament epistles. There were some pretty grievous things going on in the Corinthian church, yet the apostle Paul still called them sanctified.

What does sanctification mean? Sanctification is similar to holiness, but it means to be set apart for His service, or His purpose. When you were born again, you were sanctified by nature, which means that, in reality, there is only one use for you. You are intended to be an instrument of worship in the hands of the Master. You have no other purpose but to give Him glory and to bring Him honor.

Many people spend a lot of time and energy trying to figure out their purpose in life. Have you ever struggled with the question, "Why am I here?" If so, the simple reality is that you were created to worship Him in spirit and in truth—everything else takes a backseat. Of course, there are other things that happen in your life that are a part of God's will for you. He gives each one of us unique opportunities, gifts, and callings. But, ultimately, you can only have one core purpose in your life. Each and every thing we do should bring glory to God.

> YOU WERE CREATED TO WORSHIP HIM IN SPIRIT AND IN TRUTH—EVERYTHING ELSE TAKES A BACKSEAT.

If you are living for any other purpose, then it is time to allow your true nature to rise up and take dominion over your old man. You need to follow God's will in everything, instead of pursuing your own agenda or selfish desires. Even your job should be an act of worship to your Creator. Living each day in service to God and fulfilling His will—that is how to live a sanctified life.

You Are Eternal

Now, this characteristic of your new nature may seem a bit shocking at first. After all, while we may be accustomed to thinking of God as eternal—which He has always been and will always be—we live in a very temporal world, in a very limited body. How many times have you heard someone say, "Life is too short"? And it's true. In the natural, it seems as though one minute we are here and the next we are gone.

But the Bible says, "For the wages which sin pays is death, but the [bountiful] free gift of God is eternal life through (in union with) Jesus Christ our Lord" (Romans 6:23 AMP). You are eternal. You have been given eternal life. Death is nothing but a departure from your natural body and the beginning of a new spiritual life. Now that you are in Christ, you are continuous. Your new man has the same characteristic as Jesus Christ himself— your spirit, the real you, will never go away. You will never run out. You will never cease to be. You will never, ever experience nothingness again.

Now, this should completely alter your perspective. It should cause you to face every choice in life with one litmus test: "Does this have eternal value?" Unless you have an eye on eternity and the fact that you are going to be around forever, it's all too easy to make bad decisions and step out of the will of God. Often, the reason many believers compromise and fall into sin is because they only live in the moment. They don't want to believe that there are any consequences beyond this natural life.

But once you realize that you are eternal, your entire perspective about the way you live your life changes. Regardless of the trials and tribulations that you may face, in Christ you are able to get through anything because you can see beyond the problem and focus on the eternal purpose and promise. That's how Jesus went through the painful experience of the cross. "Looking unto Jesus the author and finisher of our faith; who for the joy that was set before him endured the cross…" (Hebrews 12:2).

When you focus on the eternal, you become kingdom minded. You seek those things which are above, and it totally changes your perspective about the value of your life. You can't be down on yourself and be eternally minded at the same time. You can't have a poor self-image or think that you're all washed up, because God is saying, "You're not done yet. You still have time. You have a purpose, and I still have some things for you to do."

You Are Love

"Beloved, let us love one another: for love is of God; and every one that loveth is born of God, and knoweth

God. He that loveth not knoweth not God; for God is love" (1 John 4:7-8). Now, this means that if you are born of God and God is love, then you are born of love. It's a part of your new nature. You are a love person. What does that mean? According to the Bible, "Love is patient, love is kind. It does not envy, it does not boast, it is not proud. It is not rude, it is not self-seeking, it is not easily angered, it keeps no record of wrongs. Love does not delight in evil but rejoices with the truth. It always protects, always trusts, always hopes, always perseveres" (1 Corinthians 13:4-7 NIV).

Obviously, that definition far exceeds any worldly understanding of love. Most of us can read this list and pick out at least one or two traits of love that are particularly difficult for us to fulfill. But that is the result of the influence of the old outer man—the soul and emotions. God's love is perfect and selfless, and that very same love has been deposited in your new nature.

For example, forgiveness is a particularly hard act of love for many people to walk in. Perhaps you have been hurt by a family member or you experience regular conflict with someone at work. We all face hurtful moments in our close relationships and interaction with acquaintances…and sometimes even with strangers. You may have a hard time forgiving those people, but that is the result of your feelings. Your soul tells you one thing—usually how much you have been wronged—while the new inner man says, "I have the ability, and I will take the opportunity, to forgive because I'm born of love. It is not my nature to hold onto unforgiveness."

> EVERY ONE OF US HAS THE ABILITY TO LOVE AND FORGIVE, REGARDLESS OF WHAT HAS HAPPENED TO US.

You are a forgiver by nature because you are born of love. Any lack of forgiveness is not the real you—that is your soul, your feelings. Every one of us has the ability to love and forgive, regardless of what has happened to us. If that weren't so, God could not hold us accountable for forgiveness. "But if ye do not forgive, neither will your Father which is in heaven forgive your trespasses" (Mark 11:26). If it were not possible to forgive, how could He ask us to do it and hold us responsible for doing it? The Word of God will separate you from your feelings and allow you to walk in the nature of your new man. You will be able to love people when they are unlovely. You will love people who don't love you in return. You will have the ability to forgive people when they hurt you. You are more than able to deal with anything because you are born of love.

You Bear His Fruit

The Bible says, "But the fruit of the Spirit is love, joy, peace, longsuffering, gentleness, goodness, faith, meekness, temperance: against such there is no law. And they that are Christ's have crucified the flesh with the affections and lusts. If we live in the Spirit, let us also walk in the Spirit" (Galatians 5:22-25).

This scripture is saying that if you belong to Christ, then the Holy Spirit is working through your spirit to produce its own fruit. Now, look at that list very closely. If you live and walk in the Spirit, this is what your life is going to look like because this is the real you. If there's something else happening, it's not coming out of your spirit. It's not your true nature. It's not coming from the Christ-man, it's coming from your flesh.

If simply allowed to grow, these traits—and more—will develop and become evident in your life. Now, these characteristics are like a genetic blueprint. Just like a natural seed, the qualities inherent in the seed begin to release as growth occurs. If you plant a tomato seed, you aren't going to get a rosebush. That seed you planted will grow and produce tomatoes just like the one that gave you the seed.

Well, it's exactly the same way with the seed of Christ. All the characteristics of Christ are in the seed. Nothing that Christ has put in you is bad. As you start to grow spiritually and the seed germinates, His characteristics start to come out and the fruit is released. You begin to manifest the Christ-man because you're born of Him. The fruit of the Spirit is what you become. There are no hidden curses or unwanted traits. There is no corruption in the seed. And so you can go forward in Christ with full confidence, knowing that the outcome can only be good.

> ALL OF THE CHARACTERISTICS OF CHRIST JESUS ARE CONTAINED WITHIN YOUR SPIRIT.

Every believer ought to be motivated in the deepest way to grow spiritually. Continued spiritual growth is how you overcome that outer man and bring him into subjection, exercising the dominion that is yours in Christ. You are a new creature; you have been made righteous; you have been made holy; you are sanctified and set apart for His purpose. All of the characteristics of Christ Jesus are contained within your spirit. Get excited, and fully embrace what the Word of God says about your new nature—which is the nature of Christ!

Study Guide

Human nature is not very pretty. Despite what some people would have us believe, we are not born "good." In fact it isn't long at all before human beings begin to demonstrate selfishness, rebellion, deceit, and many other sinful characteristics. Spend a day with a toddler, and it quickly becomes obvious that we are born with a natural inclination toward certain undesirable traits. Thankfully we don't have to operate with a human nature—we are given Christ's nature, perfect and blameless!

1. What does it mean to be holy? How does holiness differ from the concept of sanctification? Why is understanding your purpose in life so critical to being able to walk according to God's ways?

2. The Bible says you have been given the gift of eternal life, meaning that regardless of what happens to your physical body, you will never cease to exist. How does this affect your view of death? Does this change your approach to making decisions and choices in life? How does your daily life match up against the "eternal" litmus test?

3. The world's definition of love is very different from the reality of God's love. How does 1 Corinthians 13:4-7 define love? Do you walk in that kind of love in your relationships? How does love empower you to fulfill the godly nature of your new man?

*Unless the L*ORD *builds the house, its builders labor in vain.*

—Psalm 127:1 NIV

Chapter 5

Your New Structure

Some time ago, I had an experience that taught me an important lesson about developing the inner man. While on a trip to New York City with my family, we decided to visit some of the popular landmarks of the city, including the Statue of Liberty. So we took the ferry out to Liberty Island and joined a large crowd of people waiting to tour the Statue. Rather than waiting an hour for the elevator, we decided to walk up instead, and soon we were climbing the stairs that gave us a firsthand look at the inner workings of the monument.

Now, what surprised me the most was that the support framework we were climbing was really the same as any modern steel building, much like a skyscraper. The Statue of Liberty has appendages that stick out and steel "skin" that forms what can be seen on the outside. But, otherwise, the inner structure bears little physical resemblance to the shape of a woman. It is that unseen inner support, which has been constructed upon sound engineering principles instead of a purely "artistic" design, that has kept the statue stable and secure for hundreds of years.

Now, the Lord said to me, "People look at the 'skin' on the outside, and that is the equivalent of window dressing." For the most part, when people consider the Christian lifestyle, they only look at the outer "skin" and try to determine whether or not they can effectively carry off the appearance of holiness and righteousness. Can they give up smokin', drinkin', cussin' and fast livin'? They don't really consider what the Word of God says about the changes that are necessary in the inner man. So many believers pick and choose what teachings they will follow, ignoring parts of the Bible that are difficult or inconvenient, or that they don't understand. They think, *If everything looks good on the outside, who cares what else goes on that nobody knows about?* But that is not the way to build up your new inner man so that you can be victorious and have dominion over your old outer flesh.

> IT'S POINTLESS TO JUST GO THROUGH THE MOTIONS OF BEING A CHRISTIAN, HOPING THAT YOU "LOOK RIGHT" ON THE OUTSIDE.

Truth—in its entirety—provides the framework for a stable structure. And if you really want to walk in what Christ has for you, you have to get in there and deal with the framework instead of worrying about the outer skin. It's pointless to just go through the motions of being a Christian, hoping that you "look right" on the outside. In the long run, you won't be successful, because unless your inner man is built firmly upon the truth of God's Word, you'll always look kind of twisted. But if you get it right, then, in practice and lifestyle, you will look like what the Lord intended you to be.

Doctrine is the scriptural structure of the Truth, God's Word. *Practice*, on the other hand, is the application of the Truth. If you don't have the inner structure right, the practice is not going to be right either. So people struggle with the practice and try to effect change in their flesh, when in reality what they need to fix is the structure. Once that happens, form always follows function. You get the structure right and the form will naturally line up the way it is supposed to be.

Things in the world change with the passage of time. Cultures change, languages change, traditions of men change. This often causes the *practice* of Truth to look different from one generation to the next. But fortunately, the *structure* of the Truth never changes. The Word is forever settled in heaven. Because of this, we can lay the foundation of our new inner man one truth at a time.

Perhaps you are wondering, *Well, how do I make that a reality in my life?* The answer is only found in the Word of God. You see, it's an inside-out thing. It's the structure on the inside that holds up the statue. And you need to have a structure of doctrinal truth and life built on the inside of you that is formed by God. When you know who you are in Christ, walking in the Spirit is just very simply living from the inside out. The Christian lifestyle should not be a struggle. It shouldn't be hard to be who you were created to be. It's not difficult to follow Jesus. But you have to know who you are in order to be able to walk in the Spirit. Once you lay the foundation of truth inside your spirit, looking and acting like Christ is the most natural thing in the world, because that's who you are.

THE DOCTRINE OF THE NEW MAN

The building plan—or doctrine—for your new inner man is found in the Word of God. First, according to 2 Corinthians 5:17 NIV, ***you are a new creature***. "Therefore, if anyone is in Christ, he is a new creation; the old has gone, the new has come!" You are already a new creature, but you can't see the difference in the mirror. It isn't visible to those around you either, because the inner man is where you have been changed. According to the Word, He has given you a new spirit and a new heart. Hallelujah!

Secondly, we know that ***the old man is dead***. "For we know that our old self was crucified with him so that the body of sin might be done away with, that we should no longer be slaves to sin—because anyone who has died has been freed from sin" (Romans 6:6-7 NIV). Your old man was crucified with Christ; therefore your old nature is dead and you have been freed from sin.

> YOUR NEW INNER MAN IS GOING TO HAVE TO RETRAIN YOUR FLESH AND CHANGE HIS WAYS.

Now, it's true that your flesh remembers how to act like a sinner. All that means is that your outer man has muscle memory. Your new inner man is going to have to retrain your flesh and change his ways. But the only way that will happen is if you allow the resurrection power that is on the inside of you to rise up and take dominion. Forget about looking at your actions. The new structure on the inside of you is built on what the Bible says. Your actions are not the truth. The Word of God is Truth. You begin by receiving what the Word says, and then you are able to do the Word. So rejoice! Don't cry. Don't sit around weeping and have a funeral for your old self. It's already over and done. Even if you can't see it, you are better off without that old man.

The next cornerstone of the new inner man is that ***you are already in the Spirit***. Romans 8:9 says, "But ye are not in the flesh, but in the Spirit, if so be that the Spirit of God dwell in you." This is talking about your nature. You are not living in the flesh anymore. You are in the Spirit. Now, if you're walking in the flesh, that means you aren't acting according to what you were created to be. That is the difference between doctrine and practice. But remember, we have to start with doctrine. And, according to the Word of God, doctrine says that you are seated with Christ in heavenly places. You are no longer of the flesh; you are in the Spirit.

Once you are in the Spirit, you should live in the Spirit. The Bible says, "If ye then be risen with Christ, seek those things which are above, where Christ sitteth on the right hand of God" (Colossians 3:1). Notice again the present tense: "If ye then *be* risen with Christ." Not later, but *now* we are risen with Christ. So our lives should be focused toward heavenly things. "Set your affection on things above, not on things on the earth. For ye are dead, and your life is hid with Christ in God" (Colossians 3:2-3).

The next point follows closely: ***Walking in the Spirit is how you deal with the flesh***. When it comes to controlling the flesh, you have a choice. You can either resort to religion, which is structure applied to the outer man in an attempt to restrain him, or you can walk in the Spirit and rely on the truth to bring your flesh into submission. "This I say then, Walk in the Spirit, and ye shall not fulfill the lust of the flesh.

For the flesh lusteth against the Spirit, and the Spirit against the flesh: and these are contrary the one to the other: so that ye cannot do the things that ye would. But if ye be led of the Spirit, ye are not under the law" (Galatians 5:16-18).

If your flesh suddenly breaks loose, lashing religion—or the law—around it and attempting to reign it in is only going to mask the problem. And rarely is it very effective. In those situations we have to seek the Lord for wisdom as to how sin was allowed to rise up in our flesh in the first place. And He will show us what we did—what dominion we yielded—that caused us to lose spiritual control of the outer man. "Walk in the Spirit, and ye shall not fulfill the lust of the flesh." Notice that this scripture does not say, "restrain the flesh and you'll be in the Spirit." That's religion. This doesn't mean that you should just allow your flesh free reign. No, you stop it, but you stop it spiritually.

Walking in the Spirit begins with acknowledging the fact that you are in the Spirit. You aren't trying to become something that you're not. You are a new creature, and therefore you act like one. You take dominion over the outer man and make him do what he's supposed to do—from the inside out. Perhaps you are thinking, *That sounds like willpower.* No, it's simply a matter of getting your will lined up with the Word. When you renew your mind according to the Spirit, you are then able to let the Spirit of God dictate what your will does.

Finally, the last doctrinal truth is critical: ***Building up the inner man guarantees dominance of the flesh***. We know that external control, in the form of religion, is ineffective at best when it comes to controlling the sinful habits of the outer man. But building up the inner man automatically results in exercising dominion over the flesh. You have to train your inner man to rise up and say, "Well, I know who I am, so pay attention, body and mind—this is the way we're going to go. We're going to serve God now. Body and mind—you are going to get in line. You're going to do what I say, in the name of Jesus."

Sin is like a snowball rolling down a hill. It gains momentum and takes control of everything. It becomes totally unpredictable and uncontrollable. But the blood of Jesus has authority over sin. Now, what happens when the blood of Jesus is applied? The power of sin is broken, which returns dominion to you. It puts you back in control again, instead of something else controlling you.

> YOUR NEW SPIRIT ALREADY HAS THE CHARACTERISTICS OF DOMINION, AUTHORITY, AND POWER.

You see, you are a ruler by nature. Your new spirit already has the characteristics of dominion, authority, and power. That is why things are out of order when your flesh tries to dominate you—it's backward. In those situations, the enemy is trying to get your spirit to surrender its rightful authority. If you allow your flesh to come under the control of the enemy, he will turn your flesh against you and bring you into bondage. So you have no choice but to exercise dominion over yourself.

Fortunately, there is nothing about your spiritual man that you want to hinder. There is nothing innately bad or sinful to worry about, for your new nature is created after the image of Christ. So growing up spiritually is only going to bless you. It's going to give you victory and success. It's not going to hurt you or cause you to fail.

Second Corinthians 4:16 says, "For which cause we faint not; but though our outward man perish, yet the inward man is renewed day by day." You see, the outer man will eventually lose out in favor of the inner man if you are faithful to build up that inner man. According to the Word, your outer man is dead already. So rising up spiritually and taking dominion is how you will be able to exercise the control that you need to live the Christian lifestyle.

How do you build up the inner man? Well, it's an exercise of the Word and Spirit. You have to feed on the Word of God—that inner man is hungry. He wants the Word. He wants to pray. He wants to worship God. The more contact your inner man has with Jesus, with the Spirit of God, and with the Word of God, the stronger he's going to get. The structure of your inner man will be so unshakeable that you will be able to stand against any test and trial the enemy brings against you. You'll be like the wise man Jesus spoke of, who built his foundation upon the Word, "And the rain descended, and the floods came, and the winds blew, and beat upon that house; and it fell not" (Matthew 7:25).

Study Guide

How do you build something that will stand the test of time? Any builder will tell you that the foundation is critical, and so is the integrity of the framework. Without a sturdy structure, at some point everything will come tumbling down. The only way to build your life is on the truth of God's Word!

1. If the old man is dead once we accept Christ, why do we still struggle with the same sins and issues? How can your inner man gain control of the outer flesh? Why do some Christians seem to prefer their old ways and lifestyle? How do you establish a strong structure in the inner man? What effect does that have on the way your life appears to others?

2. What does it mean to "live in the Spirit"? How do you build up, or strengthen, the inner man? Does religion help or hinder your efforts?

Part II

Your New Life

Thus saith the LORD of hosts, the God of Israel, Amend your ways and your doings, and I will cause you to dwell in this place.

—Jeremiah 7:3

The old order changeth, yielding place to new. And God fulfils himself in many ways, Lest one good custom should corrupt the world.

—Alfred Tennyson

Chapter 6

Power for Life

The Bible says, "You were taught, with regard to your former way of life, to put off your old self, which is being corrupted by its deceitful desires; to be made new in the attitude of your minds; and to put on the new self, created to be like God in true righteousness and holiness" (Ephesians 4:22-24 NIV). In other words, get rid of the old man and his entire way of life. Stop thinking like the old man, stop acting like the old man, and stop living like the old man.

Now, it is important to realize that the book of Ephesians was written to Christians. It was written to the church in Ephesus, and it is written to you. So why would the apostle Paul tell them to put on the new man? Aren't we already the new man according to our faith in Christ? The Bible says, "Therefore if any man *be* in Christ, *he is* a new creature: old things are passed away; behold, all things are become new" (2 Corinthians 5:17, emphasis added). You *are* the new man. You are a new creation. But in this context, "putting on the new self" is talking about changing your lifestyle from the old way of life to the new way in Christ. And in order to do that, you have to get your mind renewed. Renewing the spirit of your mind affects everything that is relative to who you are now in Christ.

> WALKING IN THE NEW MAN INCLUDES WHAT WE SAY, WHAT WE THINK, HOW WE ACT, AND WHAT WE DO.

It's time to put off the old lifestyle and put on the new lifestyle, which after God, is created in righteousness and true holiness. You see, walking in the new man includes what we say, what we think, how we act, and what we do. You must let go of the old. The new man is righteous and holy, for he has been created that way. That's the new you.

Now, the admonition in these verses is to change from the behavior of the old man to the new man. The new man is always going to talk about who he is, what he has in God, and where he's going. We should never lose hope because of where we're going. We should never run out because of what we have been given. And we should never get down on ourselves because of who we are. We've been made to be the righteousness of God in Christ.

A New Way of Thinking

Many years ago, right before I became born again, I was diagnosed with a terminal liver condition. I was told that I was not going to live, and as a result, I turned to God and accepted Jesus as my Savior. Miraculously, I was completely healed that day, from the top of my head to the soles of my feet. The disease was gone.

But a year later, some of the symptoms started coming back on my body. Of course, I prayed. But the Lord had me take a good look at my prayer life and showed me that I was still praying like a beggar. I was still acting like a second-class citizen because that was how I saw myself. So I began to search the Word of God to learn about who I really am in Christ. I discovered that "…with his stripes we are healed" (Isaiah 53:5). I took a good look at myself and thought, *Well, if I'm healed, why am I talking like I'm sick?* And I decided to bring about a complete renovation of my thinking, my speaking, and my acting. At that time I resolved that I would never again say with my mouth that I was sick. I renewed the spirit of my mind, and because of that I now walk in divine health.

Another thing that had to change was my thinking concerning finances and provision. Growing up, I was always told that we were poor. Or, more accurately according to the southern tradition, we were "po' folks." And I believed it. It became a part of my identity. When I found out that in Christ I was rich, I didn't have two nickels to rub together. But the Word says, "My God shall supply all your need according to his riches in glory by Christ Jesus" (Philippians 4:19). So I had to change my thinking and change the words that I spoke about myself. I had to stop saying anything that even suggested that I didn't have enough. And, as a result, all of my needs have been and are met!

> THE WORD GIVES THAT OLD MAN A COMPLETE LIFESTYLE CHANGE—YOU GET AN EXTREME MAKEOVER!

My old man was sick unto death, but my new man is healed by the blood of Jesus. I may have been raised poor, but I am not poor. I was bound before I got saved, but I'm no longer bound. I had a terrible life, but now I've got a good life. The good news for all of us is that this is just the tip of the iceberg! From here on out, it only gets better. The Word gives that old man a complete lifestyle change—you get an extreme makeover!

FREEDOM FROM THE LAW

We know that according to the Word of God, man is a spirit, has a soul, and lives in a body. We've learned that our true nature is contained within our spirit—that is the source of life. Without the spirit, the body would be lifeless.

When we are born again, we receive a completely new spirit. That is the reality of who we are now in Christ. But that old nature still has some residual influence over your life. Your old spirit lived through your body and your mind and it left behind the old ways. Your mind still thinks like it used to think, unless it's been renewed by the power of God. Your body still remembers the old sinful behaviors. Those old ways are a learned pattern left over from the old nature. But now you are connected to a new life source.

Your new spirit man is like one of those old coal-burning locomotives. As someone fed the engine coal and stoked the fire in the boiler, it eventually got hot enough to produce the power necessary to pull the train. In the same way, as you feed your spirit man, stoking the fire with the Word of God, soon enough power will be produced to pull you out of that old dead junk. It literally pulls you out of darkness and into the light.

First Corinthians 15:56 says, "The sting of death is sin; and the strength of sin is the law." This scripture is referring to the Old Testament Mosaic law, but it's also talking about a mentality that relies on dead works. Unfortunately, in the body of Christ today, there are many Christians trying to live according to religious traditions rather than the Word of God. They think that Christianity is about serving a code. They set aside the Word and, instead, commit themselves to a code of conduct.

It was never God's intention to bring bondage with the law, but until Jesus came and offered himself as a perfect, living sacrifice, there was no other way to deal with mankind's sin. The law actually gives sin the power to condemn you, because no one other than Jesus can actually fulfill it. The Bible says, "For all have sinned, and come short of the glory of God" (Romans 3:23). No matter how hard the people tried to fulfill the law under the old covenant, no one ever was perfect enough. No one was made righteous. As a result, attempting to keep the law inevitably resulted in condemnation because they never fully achieved it. And now the whole mentality and tradition of the law has come over into the New Testament church. People are attempting to live the Old Testament way—through the traditions of men, which don't have any life in them. It's called dead works. And trying to serve God with dead works only produces bondage.

Condemnation is a fruit of the law, and condemnation will only bring you back into bondage. Many Christians are controlled by a sense of guilt or obligation. But the Bible says, "There is therefore now no condemnation to them which are in Christ Jesus, who walk not after the flesh, but after the Spirit" (Romans 8:1). So if you are in Christ Jesus, there is no condemnation for you. Even if you make a mistake and get into sin, you are still not condemned.

> CONDEMNATION IS A FRUIT OF THE LAW, AND CONDEMNATION WILL ONLY BRING YOU BACK INTO BONDAGE.

"For the law of the Spirit of life in Christ Jesus hath made me free from the law of sin and death" (Romans 8:2). Thank God, we don't have to live up to the unattainable standard of the old covenant! If I make a mistake, God is not going to reject me. He draws me to himself through the conviction of the Holy Spirit, but He never condemns me. My faith connects with His mercy. I ask for forgiveness, and He washes away my sin.

We have to understand that there is no power in religion. Only the blood of Jesus breaks the power of sin. Willpower isn't enough. The things that you do in the flesh aren't enough. Only the law of the Spirit of life in Christ Jesus can make us free from the law of sin and death. It lifts us out of our sin and circumstances. It gives us the power to live. We are able to go on and overcome. We are set free! The last thing I want to do is to go back and try to live by the law or the religious traditions of men. Why would I let that bring me into bondage when I've been set free? We are free!

The Power of the Word

To attempt to overcome sin and carnality by tying your flesh down with religious rigor will only put you into greater bondage. The new man must be allowed to express himself and live through the body in order to bring the flesh into obedience. Remember that your spirit is like a dynamo of heat and power. When you rise up spiritually and take dominion over that outer man, it purges out the old dark ways, and newness comes.

The secret is learning how to release the power of God in your life so that your physical body is actually changed or transformed out of the old way and into the new. "But if the Spirit of him that raised up Jesus from the dead dwell in you, he that raised up Christ from the dead shall also quicken your mortal bodies by his Spirit that dwelleth in you. Therefore, brethren, we are debtors, not to the flesh, to live after the flesh. For if ye live after the flesh, ye shall die: but if ye through the Spirit do mortify the deeds of the body, ye shall live" (Romans 8:11-13). Notice that we put to death the deeds of the body *by the Spirit*, rather than by the law. The Bible also says, "Let not sin therefore reign in your mortal body, that ye should obey it in the lusts thereof. Neither yield ye your members as instruments of unrighteousness unto sin: but yield yourselves unto God, as those that are alive from the dead, and your members as instruments of righteousness unto God" (Romans 6:12-13).

Jesus said you need the Word of God rather than tradition. Tradition binds. It's nothing more than dead works. But the Word of God, the Spirit of God, produces life. If you choose the Word, the power of the Spirit of God will purge out the old ways. Resurrection power will drive darkness out of your body, but you have to yield yourself to the Word in order for that to happen. You have to yield to works of righteousness rather than works of the law.

How do we actually apply this in real life? We can use marriage as a good example. You see, the New Testament gives plenty of instruction on how to live in a Christian marriage. If we take the Word of God and lend our members to it, acting on the Word instead of on tradition, then we are able to draw on life-giving power, and our marriages will be renewed. On the other hand, if we are acting according to something other than the Word, there is no life-changing power, and our relationships will continue to struggle in the old ways of the flesh.

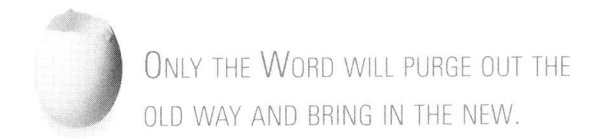

> ONLY THE WORD WILL PURGE OUT THE OLD WAY AND BRING IN THE NEW.

Perhaps your parents had a strong marriage, and you try to conduct your own relationship after the example they set for you. Unfortunately, there's no life in that. Your parents may have had a marriage that many would envy, but there is no power in tradition even if it seems to be a good thing. Power is only in the Word. If you want God in your marriage, if you want your outer man to be purged and give forth life, then you have to take the Word and make that the standard you live by. Only the Word will purge out the old way and bring in the new.

Another good example is how you make your living. The Bible is clear about how we should work and labor as unto the Lord. But if you leave that area of your life to your own thinking; if you rely solely on your education; if you are influenced by how the world says you should approach your job, you won't have newness of life in that area of your life. The only way to draw on the power of your new man is to apply the Word of God in every situation you encounter in the workplace. Anything else is fruitless in the kingdom of God.

What this means is that instead of laboring in the traditions of men and performing dead works, we walk in truth and perform works of righteousness. The Word gives direction that applies to every area of your life. But if you don't take the Word and act on it, you will never escape the corruption of the old man. You have to make the decision that you are no longer going to live by tradition; you will no longer slave under the law and condemnation; you will no longer live the old life. Instead, you turn to the Word of God and learn how to walk in His ways. You learn how to nurture your relationship with God. You learn how to serve the body in the church and to be a minister and ambassador for Christ. You learn how to be a godly husband or wife. You learn how to be a blessing. You learn how to serve your employer as unto the Lord. And before you know it, the power that is released in your new man pulls you right out of the old, miserable life you used to live into a new life full of freedom, dominion, and victory.

Study Guide

Too many Christians are walking around defeated. Sickness, poverty, and divorce are as prevalent in the church as in the world…sometimes worse. What effect might the body of Christ have on the world if they really caught hold of the truth of what Jesus has given them? The power of God is yours for the taking—power to live free from sickness, defeat, and discouragement!

1. How does your mindset have to change when you become new in Christ? Do you struggle with feelings of unworthiness or guilt? How might a new revelation of who you really are revolutionize your life? Are you excited about who you are in Christ and what God is doing, or do you dread the future?

2. How has the "law" mentality affected the New Testament church? Is it really God's desire that you labor under the bondage of a set of rules and regulations? Why is the law of the Spirit of life in Christ Jesus a better standard by which to live?

3. Are the traditions of man and the church beneficial or destructive? Why can living according to tradition be dangerous? If the traditions of men lack the power you need, what source should you draw from?

I believe that man will not merely endure. He will prevail. He is immortal, not because he alone among creatures has an inexhaustible voice, but because he has a soul, a spirit capable of compassion and sacrifice and endurance.

—William Faulkner

CHAPTER 7

THE POWER WALK

THE IDEA OF WALKING IN FREEDOM AND VICTORY may seem like an impossible dream sometimes. We all face challenges in life—some serious, while others may be less significant. But few of us experience the level of persecution and suffering that the apostle Paul and those close to him had to endure: they were thrown in prison, stoned, shipwrecked, and beaten—all for proclaiming the good news of Jesus Christ. Now *that* would be a bad day! But even while facing these dire circumstances, Paul wrote the following to the Corinthian church:

Knowing that he which raised up the Lord Jesus shall raise up us also by Jesus, and shall present us with you. For all things are for your sakes, that the abundant grace might through the thanksgiving of many redound to the glory of God. For which cause we faint not; but though our outward man perish, yet the inward man is renewed day by day. For our light affliction, which is but for a moment, worketh for us a far more exceeding and eternal weight of glory; while we look not at the things which are seen, but at the things which are not seen: for the things which are seen are temporal; but the things which are not seen are eternal.
—2 Corinthians 4:14-18

Despite every impossible circumstance in the natural realm, Paul is basically saying, "They can't touch my inner man. This situation is only temporary—I won't give up!" What kind of faith can declare prison, torture, and beatings as nothing more than a "light affliction"? Paul was able to proclaim that truth because he was speaking from a position of victory. He knew that regardless of what they tried to do to his outer man, his inward man was renewed every day.

His external circumstances were nothing compared to the power that God had placed within him. He saw the prize that was worth dying for, and he knew who would win in the end!

Perhaps you have faced all kinds of terrible things, and you feel as though you've been stoned and beaten or thrown in prison. The difference between being held down by your circumstances or being on top of them is the power of the Holy Spirit. We have to learn how to activate that power in our lives—even in the face of terrible circumstances.

Power That is Eternal

Have you ever been on a power walk? For many years, fitness experts have recommended walking as the best form of exercise to improve your stamina and overall health. Just adding thirty minutes of walking a day is supposed to be enough to dramatically improve your cardiovascular health. But unlike a leisurely stroll or even a well-paced jaunt around the neighborhood, a power walk is an exercise in strength and endurance, combined with speed. Arms pumping, feet always making contact with the ground in a heel-to-toe motion, the right posture, and even carrying small weights make the activity an intense physical workout that both builds and demonstrates the *power* in our physical bodies.

In a similar way, a spiritual power walk is when a believer rises up and says, "I'm going to live every day in this power that I know is mine. I'm not going to be overcome by bad attitudes, and I'm not going to be affected by circumstances. I am going to hold my head up and walk powerfully with God." This believer is not just along for the ride or halfheartedly living the Christian life—he is determined to walk with strength and purpose. Jesus said "He that believeth on me, as the scripture hath said, out of his belly shall flow rivers of living water" (John 7:38). Jesus was referring to the inner man, the power source of your life, the real you—your spirit.

Look again at what Paul wrote in 2 Corinthians 4:18 ASV: "While we look not at the things which are seen, but at the things which are not seen: for the things which are seen are temporal; but the things which are not seen are eternal." This scripture is a spiritual paradox. How can you not look at things which are easily seen, yet see something that you can't see? Paul is talking about two different worlds. He's talking about the difference between your outer man and inner man. He's talking about the natural, physical world and the spiritual realm that is all around us. He's talking about angels. He's talking about God. He's saying that what really counts is not in the physical realm. The real power of life is contained within the spiritual realm—those things will endure forever, long after this physical world has faded away.

SUBDUE THE FLESH

The secret to walking in power is learning how to stay out of the flesh. Many times, when I wake up on Sunday mornings, I need a major attitude adjustment. At 5:50 in the morning, when my alarm goes off and I swing my feet out of bed, my flesh is not usually very happy. But I get in the shower and turn on the hot water, and by the time I get my head wet, I've started to sing to the Lord. Sometimes I have to consciously decide to praise Him on purpose. But it doesn't take long before something starts welling up out of my spirit on the inside of me. By the time I get done with my shower, my flesh is subdued, and I'm walking in life and power.

Another example of how I have learned to overcome my flesh involves my physical immune system. When

I started traveling a lot overseas, I discovered that there are parts of the world where sickness and disease exist like we have never seen before here in America. Most of us haven't been subjected to the viruses and communicable diseases that are common in other parts of the world. In my early travels, I struggled fiercely every time I went overseas, but now I come and go with no ill effects whatsoever. This is both a natural thing and a supernatural thing. I learned where I needed to focus my faith and, at the same time, my immune system has been built up in the natural. Now I can go to places that are plagued with sickness and disease without experiencing any adverse effects.

We all have a spiritual immune system. When it is depleted or weakened, your circumstances can make it seem as though the end is near because you don't have any strength left to fight. But the book of Proverbs says, "The spirit of a man will sustain his infirmity" (Proverbs 18:14). When you are built up spiritually, your inner man can become so strong that it just overpowers the physical weaknesses in your body.

The principle here is that there are things we can do that will get the inner man up and moving and in control of that outer man. That outer man might be perishing, but your inner man is renewed day by day. Your "energy reserves" are inexhaustible—they will never run dry. The power and the glory of God is within you, and you are connected to a power source that never fails.

> THE POINT OF THE POWER WALK IS GETTING THE POWER OF GOD OUT OF YOUR SPIRIT AND INTO YOUR OUTER MAN.

THE GLORY OF GOD

The point of the power walk is getting the power of God out of your spirit and into your outer man. How do we accomplish that? Remember, we are supposed to keep our eyes on things that we can't see—things that are eternal. The power will come when you focus on the Word and the glory of God, as well as the reflection of His glory that is in you. But how do we behold the glory? The Bible tells us:

Now if the ministry that brought death, which was engraved in letters on stone, came with glory, so that the Israelites could not look steadily at the face of Moses because of its glory, fading though it was, will not the ministry of the Spirit be even more glorious? If the ministry that condemns men is glorious, how much more glorious is the ministry that brings righteousness! For what was glorious has no glory now in comparison with the surpassing glory. And if what was fading away came with glory, how much greater is the glory of that which lasts!

Therefore, since we have such a hope, we are very bold. We are not like Moses, who would put a veil over his face to keep the Israelites from gazing at it while the radiance was fading away. But their minds were made dull, for to this day the same veil remains when the old covenant is read. It has not been removed, because only in Christ is it taken away. Even to this day when Moses is read, a veil covers their hearts. But whenever anyone turns to the Lord, the veil is taken away. Now the Lord is the Spirit, and where the Spirit of the Lord is, there is freedom. And we, who with unveiled faces all reflect the Lord's glory, are being transformed into his likeness with ever-increasing glory, which comes from the Lord, who is the Spirit.

—2 Corinthians 3:7-18 NIV

This passage of Scripture is referring to the story of Moses, who went up on Mt. Sinai and remained in the presence of God for forty days. When Moses came down off the mountain, he had the Ten Commandments, among other things, but his face was shining and radiant. Moses wasn't born again, but the glory of God still had an effect on his physical body. He had been transformed by the power of God.

When the people of Israel saw his face, they were afraid of him. They had a negative reaction to the power of God because of who they were. They were covenant people, but they weren't washed in the blood of the Lamb. Under the Old Testament, the glory of God was a terrifying thing. Because of sin, man was not worthy to be in God's presence. Just one misstep and a man would die. So when Moses came down off the mountain, the Israelites—afraid of the residual glory that still lingered on him—pleaded with him to cover his face with a veil.

That veil became both a literal and symbolic representation of the separation between God and man. Even though the people of Israel were in covenant with God, there still had to be a veil, and one was tangibly erected in the tabernacle to separate the holy of holies from the outer court so that God could dwell in the presence of the nation of Israel without killing them. But when Jesus died on the cross, the veil of the temple was rent in two, signifying that the way into the holy of holies was now made open. Under the new covenant, when you are born again, your sin is cleansed and the glory of God is not a threat to you. Frankly, you could walk directly into the presence of God, into the throne room of heaven, without any negative repercussions. The glory of God is no strange thing for you because of who you are in Christ.

So, in the same way that Moses' outer man was affected by beholding the glory on top of the mountain, you and I are able to look upon the glory of God and be forever changed. But you won't find the glory on top of Mt. Sinai or behind the temple curtain. The glory is going to come upon your outer man when you look in the mirror of God's Word that shows you that the glory is already in you.

The night before Jesus was crucified, He prayed for His disciples and said, "The glory which thou gavest me I have given them; that they may be one, even as we are one" (John 17:22). I promise you, Jesus gets His prayers answered! As His disciple, you have been glorified with the same glory with which He has been glorified. "But if the Spirit of him that raised up Jesus from the dead dwell in you, he that raised up Christ from the dead shall also quicken your mortal bodies by his Spirit that dwelleth in you" (Romans 8:11). The glory is in you.

Let's look at 2 Corinthians 3:17 NIV again: "Now the Lord is the Spirit, and where the Spirit of the Lord is, there is freedom." By contrast, the Bible tells us that the letter of the law—or religious tradition—kills. (See Romans 7:6.) Why does the law kill? Because it denies that you've been changed. The letter of the law produces condemnation because it assumes that you're still a sinner. Still trying to arrive. Still trying to work your way in. The letter kills, but the Spirit gives life.

> Making mistakes doesn't mean that you are done, because God doesn't give up on people.

New Testament living is all about who you are now and who you're growing to be. It accepts as fact that change has occurred in your inner man. That you have been glorified with Christ and that the same Spirit that raised Him from the dead is dwelling in you. Even making mistakes doesn't mean that you are done, because God doesn't give up on people. You may have a hard time believing that the glory of God is in you, but if you're saved, the Bible says it is. So you need to get into the Word and start reading and finding out who you are in Christ. The Word of God is going to tell you who you are, and it's going to reflect that glory to your inner man. Before you know it, the outer man will be changed, and you will be walking in freedom.

Turbulent Times

Most likely, you realize that we are living in very turbulent times. It would be hard not to be aware of that—every day seems to bring countless crises around the nation and the world, as the media works overtime to pump fear and division into the American public. It's a pressure cooker, and any person who is not strong in the Lord can really be swept away in all of the turmoil.

As a young man, I used to surf in Hawaii. Some of the biggest waves in the world are found in Hawaii, and one of the characteristics of those waves is that if you get in the wrong place at the wrong time, you can get pushed down. The wave will literally hold you on the bottom of the ocean floor, dragging you along until you no longer have any idea which way is up and which way is down.

If you're in turmoil today and feel as though you've lost your bearings—as though a powerful wave is sweeping you along and you don't know which way is up—you need to develop a power walk. Sometimes circumstances are hard, and bad things can happen even when you are doing everything right. Thinking that God has forsaken you, you may even get mad at Him. There have been occasions in my own life when I have been in circumstances that were so severe that I was not even able to pray at the time. So I know what it's like to feel beaten down and so disoriented that I don't know which way is up. When that happens, all kinds of terrible things begin to come to mind. That is the perfect time for a power walk.

There are three simple steps that will launch your power walk and build up the inner man and restore your equilibrium. First, ***feed on the Word of God***. You are a spirit being and you need Spirit food. Jesus said, "The words that I speak unto you, they are spirit, and they are life" (John 6:63). You need to read and feed on the Word of God to build up that inner man. Secondly, you need to ***spend time in prayer***. You need to exercise your faith before Almighty God. Prayer is really communion with God, and it builds a connection and grounds you. The good news is: because of what Jesus did at Calvary, you have instant access to the Almighty at any time, day or night. Finally, you need to ***put the Word into practice***. You need to ***do*** the Word. James 1:22 says, "But be ye doers of the word, and not hearers only, deceiving your own selves." Your faith will not grow unless you put it into action.

Until Jesus washes away your sin, there is no connection with heaven. But when that's done, you are connected to the life source again. And the power of Almighty God comes directly into your spirit. That power will hold you up and sustain you in any situation. So when you're going through trouble, remember that though the outer man perishes, your inner man is renewed every day. That's something to rejoice about!

Study Guide

Perseverance. Faith. Strength. Purpose. All of these things are necessary if you are to live in Christ with power. Only through the Holy Spirit can you triumph over the challenges of life, rather than being defeated by them. God's power is unlimited and inexhaustible, so there is no reason to feel helpless or defeated. You can overcome!

1. We all struggle with the weaknesses of the flesh in our daily lives. How does praising God change your feelings and circumstances? What other practical things can you do to "power walk" through those moments where the old man tries to regain control?

2. How do the Word of God and the glory of God affect your life? Why do you think some Christians still live as though they are separated from God? Is it possible to spend time in God's presence or studying His Word and not be changed? How does communing with God help you overcome in times of trouble?

Sow to yourselves in righteousness, reap in mercy; break up your fallow ground: for it is time to seek the L*ORD, till he come and rain righteousness upon you.*

—Hosea 10:12

Chapter 8

The Power Principle

Do you ever wonder what really makes the world go 'round? Scientists have theories about everything from evolution to global warming, but the one fundamental truth that can accurately predict the outcome in every situation is summed up by this scripture: "Be not deceived; God is not mocked: for whatsoever a man soweth, that shall he also reap" (Galatians 6:7). That statement is the universal law of creation. Specifically, that means everything produces after its own kind.

God has established many laws that govern this realm in which we live. Some are natural laws and some are spiritual laws. Most people are familiar with the natural law of gravity: what goes up must come down. There is no real way to escape the effect of gravity on this earth, no matter how much we might want to. But the law of creation happens to be a spiritual law that also plays out in the natural, and it is very simple: whatever you sow, you will also reap. Every seed sown, or every deed done, produces after its own kind. The principle is inescapable—there is no way to get around it or avoid it.

Now, it's easy to understand and visualize the concept of a natural seed producing after itself. But this scripture is not only addressing this law in the literal sense—such as a crop of wheat that you might plant in a field—but deals with the consequences of what we ***do***. "God is not mocked" really means that God is the judge of everything. Whatever is sown has to be balanced by what is reaped, and God has ordained that every seed should produce after itself when it is sown. So whether it is an attitude, a word spoken, or a deed done, God has obligated himself to make sure that the principle of reaping comes to pass. ***Everything*** that you do has a consequence. Whether positive or negative, every action has a corresponding reaction.

> *EVERYTHING* THAT YOU DO HAS A CONSEQUENCE.

Many times people find themselves in dire circumstances and wonder, *Why is this happening to me?* The Word of God says that somewhere, somehow you sowed this and now you are reaping it (see Galatians 6:7). Sometimes it may be difficult to pinpoint where the exact seed that produced fruit was sown. After all, just because someone breaks into your home and steals from you doesn't necessarily mean that at some earlier time you stole from someone else. You may not have done the exact same thing in the exact same way, but somehow you sowed a seed that opened the door and caused this to happen in your life.

At the same time, some people think they can do whatever they want and it won't affect them. They sow their "wild oats," seemingly without consequence. Or perhaps you wonder about someone who seems to prosper, despite walking in sin or having a lack of integrity. Our society is filled with celebrities and pseudo-celebrities who live abominable lifestyles and yet seem to have everything going their way. But, rest assured, whether we see it or not or whether it is immediately apparent or not, there is no escaping the fulfillment of this law. Why? Because God is a righteous judge.

SEEDS OF THE FLESH

We know, according to the Word of God, that as believers we are made new creatures in Christ. We are washed in the blood of the Lamb. We've been delivered from the power of darkness and translated into the kingdom of His dear Son. The blessings of God belong to us because of who we are in Him. But the Bible is very clear that once you become born again, your actions and behavior have to change. Galatians goes on to say, "For he that soweth to his flesh shall of the flesh reap corruption; but he that soweth to the Spirit shall of the Spirit reap life everlasting" (Galatians 6:8).

You see, your old nature was programmed to sow seeds of destruction, seeds of sin. And although your inner man has been given a new nature through faith in Christ, your outer man has to be renewed as well or you will continue to reap the same fruit. "For they that are after the flesh do mind the things of the flesh; but they that are after the Spirit the things of the Spirit. For to be carnally minded is death; but to be spiritually minded is life and peace" (Romans 8:5-6). If you continue to walk in those old ways, if you are carnally minded and sow seeds of the flesh, you will continue to reap the fruit of sin, which is corruption and death.

Is there any possibility that you can sow a bad seed and avoid reaping from it just because you are a believer? No, being born again does not supersede the power of this law in action. You still reap what you sow. There's only one answer, and that is repentance. Otherwise it will happen to you, just like it happens to any unbeliever. You sow it, you reap it. But thank God, "The law of the Spirit of life in Christ Jesus hath made me free from the law of sin and death" (Romans 8:2). Because there is no condemnation for those who are in Christ Jesus, when we realize that we've made a mistake, God doesn't condemn us for it. But we still have to repent. If we don't repent, we're going to pay the price. God is no respecter of persons— the universal law of creation works every time.

THE BLAME GAME

When I was a young believer, I heard teachings about the principle of sowing and reaping, but when it came to my own actions I really didn't pay much attention. Then I would make a mistake, say something that I shouldn't say, or have an attitude that wasn't right. And before long I would find myself standing in the middle of a crisis, saying, "Lord! This isn't fair!" It took me a while to realize that I was reaping what I had sowed. At the time I didn't know exactly what it was that I had done, but I realized I had to be reaping ***something***, because the Word is true. The turning point came when I began to ask the Lord to show me what I was doing that was causing these things to happen. He was faithful to reveal those issues that—although I wasn't even aware of them—were producing corrupt fruit in my life.

Now, Satan, who has the very nature of deception, tries to convince us that the sowing is unrelated to the reaping; that they are completely separate incidents. When people are sowing seeds of the flesh, they don't ever consider that they will eventually have to pay for those actions. And then when they do, they don't realize that it's because of what they did. The enemy whispers in their ear, "Isn't this unfair? God really shouldn't have let this happen to you. He's supposed to protect you." Or better yet, someone will say, "Well, God must

> SO OFTEN PEOPLE BLAME GOD FOR WHAT THEY HAVE BROUGHT UPON THEMSELVES.

have some purpose in this." And what happens so often is that people blame God for what they have brought upon themselves. And the enemy—who tempted us to sin in the first place—stands there laughing at our ignorance.

If we want to change the nature of the harvest we are reaping in our lives from one of death and destruction to one of blessing and abundance, the first thing that we have to do is stop blaming God. He didn't make those choices. He didn't sow those seeds. Instead of trying to make God the problem, we must turn to Him and confess our sin and ask for forgiveness. We need to ask for wisdom and discernment to realize where we are missing it, and the strength to change the behavior of our outer man, so that we can begin to sow only seeds that will bear righteous fruit in our lives.

That is what it means to walk in humility and with a spirit of repentance. As long as we continue to make excuses, we are exhibiting behavior that is a sure sign that we haven't really repented. When a person truly repents of something, the blame game is over. The only way to dig up those seeds of the flesh and prevent them from coming to fruition is through the blood of Jesus. Only heartfelt repentance and the application of the blood of Jesus over our lives can stop the universal law of creation. That is the only way out.

THE FRUIT OF THE SPIRIT

How do we determine those things in our lives that need to change? Certainly, some issues are more obvious than others. But the Bible is very clear about which actions are after the flesh and which are not: "The acts of the sinful nature are obvious: sexual immorality, impurity and debauchery; idolatry and witchcraft; hatred, discord, jealousy, fits of rage, selfish ambition, dissensions, factions and envy; drunkenness, orgies, and the like. I warn you, as I did before, that those who live like this will not inherit the kingdom of God" (Galatians 5:19-21 NIV). Perhaps you've never had an affair, but have you flirted with the possibility? Have you entertained impure thoughts or allowed yourself to "just look" at something that is unholy? Have you engaged in the latest office gossip or spoken words of judgment and criticism about someone else? Do you covet material things? Most likely, you can identify with something on this list, because we all were born with a sinful nature and we all have struggled in one way or another with the temptations of the flesh.

But our new man is supposed to have the nature of Jesus Christ. How do we judge our actions according to the Spirit? By the fruit that we bear: "But the fruit of the Spirit is love, joy, peace, patience, kindness, goodness, faithfulness, gentleness and self-control. Against such things there is no law. Those who belong to Christ Jesus have crucified the sinful nature with its passions and desires. Since we live by the Spirit, let us keep in step with the Spirit. Let us not become conceited, provoking and envying each other" (Galatians 5:22-26 NIV). We must test every thought, word, and deed according to the fruit of the Spirit. Are our thoughts centered on Christ and His righteousness? Do the words that we speak bring blessing or cursing? Are we kind to other people, or do we react harshly? Do we think of others first, or do we pursue selfish desires?

> IF WE CONSIDER WHAT WE SAY AND DO, IT REALLY ISN'T HARD TO SEE WHICH SIDE OF THE FENCE WE ARE SOWING ON.

Do the choices we make produce peace and joy in our lives? If we take the time to consider what we say and do, it really isn't hard to see which side of the fence we are sowing on.

Jesus had a lot to say about fruit, including "Make a tree good and its fruit will be good, or make a tree bad and its fruit will be bad, for a tree is recognized by its fruit" (Matthew 12:33 NIV). In other words, it really is the way it looks. If it walks like a dog and talks like a dog, it's a dog. If it looks bad and you sow it, the harvest is going to be bad. Ever since the infamous Tree of Life in the Garden of Eden, Satan has contradicted God's Word by telling mankind that, "It's really not a bad thing at all. What's wrong with having a little fun?" And our ears start to perk up because he certainly makes it sound appealing. But the whole time God is warning us, saying "Don't sow that seed. The fruit is going to hurt. Don't do it."

Now, we have all sinned and fallen short of the glory of God. We've all sown seeds of the flesh at one time or another. This isn't about condemnation or pursuing religious works to try and atone for the past—it's about the life-changing power of the Word of God. He woos our hearts and encourages our inner man, saying, "You don't have to do that. You have the ability and power to change." He works patiently in our lives to bring us to the point where we finally decide that we don't want to live the same way anymore. And the good news is that because of who we are in Christ, we ***can*** stop sowing the wrong seed.

ACCESSING THE POWER

There isn't a believer alive who isn't able to produce the fruit of the Spirit. If it comes out of the inside of you, out of your new inner man acting on the Word of God, it is going to bear good fruit. And the purpose for the fruit is the testimony it produces in your life. The fruit always bears witness of the tree, and it confirms the nature God has placed within you. Now, when you sow bad seed, it goes against your new nature, but you did sow the seed and the fruit that results bears witness to your old man. In those moments, the enemy loves to torment you with judgment, guilt, and condemnation. That is why repentance is so important. Satan is silenced when you turn to Jesus and say, "Lord Jesus, I made a mistake, and the devil is trying to condemn me with this. He's trying to say that this is really the way I am. And Lord, You said otherwise. You said that I am a new creature. You said that old things are passed away. So, Lord Jesus, I don't receive this condemnation. I was wrong, but I ask You to forgive me."

The Bible says, "Death and life are in the power of the tongue: and they that love it shall eat the fruit thereof" (Proverbs 18:21). What you say determines how you act, so how do you get out of a bad behavior pattern? Well, if your tongue doesn't change, you won't either. The Bible says that your body—the outer man—is following your tongue. You have to change what you say in order to guide your life into productivity. You have to say with your mouth that you are a new creature—that you aren't the same person anymore…that you have the nature of Christ and, with His help, you are able to act out of the inner man.

Now, you may be dealing with some trouble right now—the consequences of what you have done in the past. But if you have sown seeds in the flesh and have not already repented before the Lord, then it is very likely that more trouble is coming. God's law is inescapable, and if you have sown in ignorance, there is a harvest coming that you don't even know about yet. The enemy has been busy trying to set you up for destruction.

How do we stop those bad seeds you've sown in the past from coming to fruition in your life? Remember, you are a new creature in Christ, and in Him there is no condemnation. Walk in humility and confess your sins before Him, and He will be faithful to forgive you. Repent for those seeds that you have sown knowingly as well as those that you may not be aware of, and the blood of Jesus will set you free from the consequences of your sin. Then ask Him to teach you how to sow the right seeds in your life. If you do this, you will benefit from the power contained within the universal law of creation. You will reap good things because you are sowing good things.

Study Guide

Even the world can't deny its truth: *Gravity*—what goes up must come down. *Karma*—what goes around comes around. And to be more accurate—*what you sow, so shall you reap.* Really, this is good news because it gives you the ability to choose the outcome you desire. Sow seeds in the flesh, and you will reap accordingly. But repent and follow the leading of the Spirit, and the blessings of God will follow you.

1. How does the universal law of creation affect your ability to walk in the Spirit? Are there areas of your life where you have opened the door to death and destruction by sowing seeds of the flesh? How can you apply this law to your life in order to reap a good harvest?

2. Have you ever blamed God for something that was the result of your own choices and actions? Why is repentance necessary? How do you change the nature of your imminent harvest?

3. Do you struggle with any of the acts of the flesh listed in Galatians 5:19-21? Do you harbor secret, subtle sins that are undermining your ability to walk in the power of the Spirit? By contrast, how prevalent is the fruit of the Spirit in your life (Galatians 5:22)?

*Now God be praised, that
to believing souls gives light in
darkness, comfort in despair.*

—William Shakespeare

Chapter 9

The Power of Your Testimony

What is the purpose of strengthening our inner man so that we can subdue the flesh? After all, if we are going to heaven anyway, why should we have to work so hard now? Well, aside from the many blessings that we receive in our individual lives from walking in relationship with God, He also has a plan to use us to change the world: "You are the light of the world. A city on a hill cannot be hidden. Neither do people light a lamp and put it under a bowl. Instead they put it on its stand, and it gives light to everyone in the house. In the same way, let your light shine before men, that they may see your good deeds and praise your Father in heaven" (Matthew 5:14-16 NIV). It is God's desire that each one of us serve as a living testimony to His goodness and love. As we walk in obedience, subduing our flesh as new creatures in Christ, His light shines through us, revealing His power to change lives and drawing unbelievers to himself.

Now, perhaps you don't feel very much like a "light." It's easy for most of us to point out our flaws and imperfections—all of the issues that we think should disqualify us from service. But Jesus said we "***are*** the light of the world." In the same way that our inner man ***is*** a new creature through faith in Christ, we are also now His ambassadors on the earth. It has absolutely nothing to do with your feelings or preferences—like it or not, you are His light to the world!

THE SPIRITUAL REALM

It's important to remember that there are two separate worlds, or creations, on this earth. There is the family of man, the old creation of Adam that is bound by sin and death, and the family of God, the new creation established by Jesus Christ. Once we accept Christ, we become a member of the family of God and, consequently, become a light to the family of man.

At the same time, there are also two different dimensions that we are a part of—the natural realm and the spiritual realm. The natural realm includes all of the tangible realities of this earth—our earthly bodies, the physical elements of the world, even the universe that surrounds us. Then there is the spiritual realm, which we are also a part of because we are created in the image of God as a spirit being. As we grow in Christ and develop our inner man, we become more aware of the reality of the spiritual realm. But often, new believers are completely unaware that there is a whole other dimension that affects their lives—a realm that includes not only God, Jesus, the Holy Spirit, and all of the hosts of heaven, but also the enemy and his minions.

> SATAN KNOWS THE INSTANT THAT WE BECOME BORN AGAIN, BECAUSE SUDDENLY WE ARE LIT WITHIN BY THE PRESENCE OF THE HOLY SPIRIT.

Unlike most of us, Satan is acutely aware of the state of our spiritual condition and identity. He knows the instant that we become born again, because suddenly we are lit within by the presence of the Holy Spirit. Where there once was only darkness, in the spiritual realm we are alight with the glory of God, and we stick out like a sore thumb. That is why he starts attacking and coming against us as soon as we became born again.

I didn't realize that I had an enemy until the day I accepted Christ. And suddenly I sensed the presence of an opposition that I had never experienced before in my life. In time I learned that the reason for this was because my position had changed at the point of my conversion. I was no longer lost and hopeless, dying and bound by sin. I was filled with the power of God and was heir to the throne of Christ. I was now a threat to the kingdom of darkness, and Satan was intimidated by me. At the time of my salvation, I couldn't grasp what God's plans were for my life, but when Satan saw that light suddenly come on in my spirit, he was afraid—and rightly so! The enemy is equally intimidated by you. Regardless of what you think about yourself, if you are born again, you are a threat to the enemy and his kingdom.

A Light on a Hill

God chose you and me to be His light in the world. Remember, Jesus said, "Neither do people light a lamp and put it under a bowl. Instead they put it on its stand, and it gives light to everyone in the house." Guess what? God is a lot smarter than any of us. He is going to put us in a prominent position so that people can see the light and the light can affect their lives. That is the function and purpose of our testimony. This is why Jesus gave us the admonition, "Let your light shine before men." Don't try to cover up what God has done in your life. It is His desire that you openly share and reveal the light that He has placed within you so "that they may see your good deeds and praise your Father in heaven."

Unfortunately, many Christians have a love-hate relationship with prominence and attention. They want to cover the light and keep their faith a "private" thing. There are many reasons for this—some people are simply introverted by nature and are uncomfortable speaking openly. Others are concerned with how they will be perceived—they want to curry the world's favor. And still others are simply too "polite"—they actually believe that testifying to the uncompromising truth of the gospel is a taboo subject—that it is better to leave people to their own opinions and religious beliefs, even if that means they remain bound by sin and destined to perish without Jesus.

But when you become born again, God says, "Look, you have to learn how to be open with people. I'm going to set you up like a beacon—as a light on a hill. I need to use you to reach people that are in darkness. So you are going to have to forget about yourself—your privacy, your individuality, your ego, your pride—and surrender all of these things to Me so I can use you. It's not about your comfort zone, it's about My kingdom."

> THERE IS NOTHING LESS EFFECTIVE THAN A CHRISTIAN WHO SAYS ONE THING YET LIVES SOMETHING ELSE.

This makes the authenticity of our testimony extremely important. There is nothing less effective than a Christian who says one thing yet lives something else. The world views that kind of hypocrisy with disdain. We can't claim to be followers of Christ, but still act in the old patterns of the flesh. The good news is that if we honor the law of love—which simply requires that we never knowingly do something that would cause another brother in Christ to stumble—

and allow our spirit man to subdue the flesh, we can't help but reveal God's light to the world.

How can we be sure of this? It's very simple—the fruit of the Spirit cannot be hidden. Fruit grows on the outside where everyone can see it, and God uses that fruit to attract people to you. What should we be producing? "But the fruit of the Spirit is love, joy, peace, patience, kindness, goodness, faithfulness, gentleness and self-control. Against such things there is no law" (Galatians 5:22-23 NIV). In other words, there is nothing powerful enough—spirit, soul, or body—that can stop fruit from developing if a believer walks in the Spirit. It will manifest in your life; it is going to happen. There is no law or force of nature that can stop it.

Walking in the Light

The Bible says, "And because ye are sons, God hath sent forth the Spirit of his Son into your hearts, crying, Abba, Father" (Galatians 4:6 NIV). "Abba, Father" is translated as "Daddy God." And as a new creation in Christ, your natural desire is to cry out to him saying, "Daddy, I love You! I am an obedient child, and I want to serve You. I want to worship You." That is the cry of your heart because you have His Spirit on the inside of you. In other words, you have been given a heart of obedience, so that when you walk in the Spirit, you will invariably and inevitably seek to please Him and live for Him. That heart, along with the evidence of what God has done in your life—both in saving and delivering you, as well as the fruit of the Spirit that you develop as you continue to walk in the Spirit—is the "light" that God reveals to the world. He does this so that people who are lost in darkness can clearly see the testimony of what God has done for you and find their way to Truth.

Jesus said, "Everyone who does evil hates the light, and will not come into the light for fear that his deeds will be exposed. But whoever lives by the truth comes into the light, so that it may be seen plainly that what he has done has been done through God" (John 3:20-21 NIV). The Holy Spirit is going to draw you out into the light and you won't be able to live in obscurity any longer. People are going to notice you and wonder what is different about you. That means we have to start living according to another set of rules. We have to learn a new lifestyle.

The primary rule is that we must learn to walk in love. We can't allow something that we do to become a stumbling block—either to our brothers and sisters in Christ or to the people we are trying to reach. Really, we live in the proverbial glass house. Everybody knows who we are; everyone is watching to see what we do. Everything that happens in your house affects your testimony. You can't even go behind closed doors without the fruit of what you do coming out in the open.

The prospect of this kind of exposure is enough to make many Christians run for the hills. But any time you are tempted to back away from the front lines and retreat to the darkness, be forewarned—you won't find any safety there. We weren't made to hide our lights under a bushel. The only way to find true peace and rest—as well as victory—is to walk in the Light.

THE STAGES OF SPIRITUAL GROWTH

Do you realize that everything God is a part of grows? If something isn't growing, He isn't in it. This is particularly true for you and me—if He is in us, we grow. If we are walking with Him, we grow. If we are obedient to Him, we grow. God is the giver of life itself—He is the Creator, and it is impossible to separate Him from the process of growth.

There are three distinct stages of spiritual growth that can help us define what a true walk in the Spirit looks like. The first is ***Elation and Rejoicing***. When we are first born again there is a period of time that is normally characterized by unrestrained peace and joy. Often, we are more open with the people who are close to us—telling them about Jesus and what He has just done in our lives because we feel so good that nothing else matters. You are wrapped up in the arms of the Lord, He's feeding you the milk of the Word, you are surrounded by a blanket of grace, and you don't have a care in the world.

But soon the time comes when God causes you to stand on your spiritual feet, and the second stage of growth begins: ***Illumination and Preparation***. This stage is like cultivation. Your growth is exponential, but it is also a serious and sober time of consecration and deepening commitment. God takes you through a period of great preparation in which you are forced to confront and deal with personal issues. He causes you to face those things in your heart—the areas of weakness that need to be strengthened—so that you are ready to go forward and fulfill that which He called you to do from the foundation of the world.

Finally, the last stage is ***Resignation and Sacrifice***. Having learned what the will of God is for your life, you settle into a life of obedience—even to the point of death if necessary—to get the will of God done. You've discovered what it is going to take to maintain a good testimony at your job. You also know what the Lord expects of you in your personal life, in your family, in your church, and you've come to a place of acceptance and determination. You are able to say, "Lord, whatever it takes, whatever You ask, I am committed. I don't want to spend my whole life doing my own thing, only to get to the end and not have anything to show for it. My sole purpose is to fulfill Your will for my life."

I'll never forget a number of years ago when the Lord called us to start doing overseas crusades. It wasn't long before we started facing criticism for not following up with each individual who came to Christ. Frankly, when that many people get born again at one time, there's really not much you can do in the natural. How would it even be possible to confirm whether every person who responded was truly repenting before

Christ? I'm not God, and I can't see their hearts. Did that mean that we should give up on mass evangelism?

I knew what God had called me to do, and despite what others might think, or the limitations of the situation, I was determined to go ahead and do it anyway. When I stand before Jesus at the end of my life, He is going to judge me based on whether I was obedient to His will, not on what other people think about me. Eventually, we all have to reach the point where it doesn't make any difference what people think anymore. We are designed to do the will of God whether people like it or not. And once that issue is settled, walking out your testimony becomes very simple. You have peace, joy, and everything you need, and you are content because you are serving Him. That is the best way to let your light shine.

Study Guide

It may seem as though becoming the "new you" is a constant, uphill battle. Certainly, the struggle can be great at times. But the rewards are worth it! Not only do you reap the blessings of God in your life, but you are able to play an important role in God's kingdom plan. No one can do what you can do. Never underestimate the power of your testimony.

1. How does being born again affect you? Why does Satan generally bring a greater assault after you are born again than he attempted when you were unsaved? What purpose does he have in attacking you, if you already know Christ? Have you found that the spirit realm has become more "real"?

2. How does your walk and the strength of your inner man affect the effectiveness of your testimony? Why is it so important that you be transparent, open, and real about your life?

*Create in me a clean heart, O God;
and renew a right spirit within me.*

—Psalm 51:10

Chapter 10

The Power Purge

Perhaps the most exciting aspect of our new life in Christ is that God has a marvelous plan for each one of us. It is His desire that we walk in victory, and there is nothing that can stand in the way of what Jesus has done in you and me. The apostle Paul wrote:

> *I pray also that the eyes of your heart may be enlightened in order that you may know the hope to which he has called you, the riches of his glorious inheritance in the saints, and his incomparably great power for us*

who believe. That power is like the working of his mighty strength, which he exerted in Christ when he raised him from the dead and seated him at his right hand in the heavenly realms, far above all rule and authority, power and dominion, and every title that can be given, not only in the present age but also in the one to come. And God placed all things under his feet and appointed him to be head over everything for the church, which is his body, the fullness of him who fills everything in every way.
—Ephesians 1:18-23 NIV

> ALL THE WORKS OF DARKNESS ARE BENEATH HIS FEET, AND IF WE ARE LIVING IN HIM, THOSE WORKS ARE UNDER OUR FEET ALSO.

There is no sin, no sickness, no compulsion, no aberrant desire—nothing that we have or will ever deal with—that has not already been defeated by Jesus on the cross. The blood of Jesus has broken the power of all sin and, consequently, has broken all the power of darkness. All the works of darkness are beneath His feet, and if we are living in Him, those works are under our feet also.

Paul tells us that we have access to God's "incomparably great power" as believers in Christ. Sadly, there is little evidence of this at work in the church today. After all, this power is the same that raised Christ Jesus from the dead! When was the last time that power was manifested in the everyday lives of believers? It is time that we go beyond where the church has been willing to go in the past. We need to go through a process of spiritual purging through the Word of God that will move us into a new level of victory and power. Really, the process is not earth-shattering—it isn't anything particularly out of the ordinary, but it is biblical. It is revolutionary for the majority of the church today. Fortunately, through faith and obedience, each one of us can receive the truth and walk in it—which will change our lives forever!

The Effect of Darkness

The Spirit of God wants to lead the church en mass into the reality of who we are in Christ. We just have to be willing to get past playing "religion." Second Corinthians 3:18 says, "But we all, with open face beholding as in a glass the glory of the Lord, are changed into the same image from glory to glory, even as by the Spirit of the Lord." The phrase "with open face" is another way of saying that there is no barrier between God and ourselves. So this means that when we look into the mirror, which is the Word of God, it reflects our true image back to us, and as we look into it, we are changed from glory to glory. Now, what kind of a change are we talking about? Are we talking about just a change in the way we think? Or the way we talk? Yes, that is part of the work of the Spirit, but that's not all there is to it. The Word effects a much more substantive change in the core of who we are.

This is necessary because of the effect that spiritual death has had on you and me. Before we are born again, we have a spirit that is contrary to God. Now that spirit and its inherent nature of sin opened us up to be used, abused, and led by the spirit of this world, which is the spirit of darkness. Since the fall of Adam and Eve in the Garden, that spirit of darkness has been working throughout this world that God originally created to be good. "And God saw every thing that he had made, and, behold, it was very good" (Genesis 1:31). But because of sin, the spirit of darkness has been able to cause distortions in mankind, as well as in the earth itself.

Science is beginning to point out these things, and it is time for the church to wake up and pay attention. Global warming, tsunamis, earthquakes, hurricanes, the extinction of animal species, and much more are examples of the work of darkness in the earth's natural realm. Genetic mutations—or "flaws" in our DNA—are just one example of the effect the spirit of darkness has had on our actual flesh. We know that Adam was created by God—to deny that or to espouse evolution as anything more than the lie of the enemy is just foolishness. But it is equally ridiculous to deny that spiritual power—and even the fallen environment itself—can genetically alter a human being. This isn't evolution—it is the cause and effect principle set in motion by sin. It is actually a spiritual principle at work in the earth.

There are genetic traits for everything from destructive habits to diseases that are passed down from generation to generation. And although the world doesn't really understand or acknowledge the real source, or even know what to call this phenomenon, we are all affected by these generational curses from birth. This doesn't mean that we aren't responsible for the things that we do, but it does mean that we need to find an answer so we can be set free from the influence and control of these things. We can have victory over familiar spirits and temptations, walk in abundance instead of suffering from poverty, and walk in health and wholeness, rather than succumbing to sickness and death.

How does this corruption of the nature and flesh happen? What is it that is done to man that distorts him? It can only come from the spirit that's working through him. The spirit of this world controls people and causes destruction—not just in simple ways, but complicated physiological damage that is done to the person because of the works of darkness.

But the good news is that the same principle applies from the side of righteousness. If God changes the spirit man, and that man is subject to the Holy Spirit—the very same Spirit that raised Jesus from the dead in power—then He works to restore those things in you that the enemy has stolen, corrupted, and perverted. The Holy Spirit works all of that destructive change in the opposite direction and empowers you to act out the things of God. He begins to transform your life to the point that you are who God originally intended you to be—restoring that which God created "good" before sin entered the world. We are not without hope in this

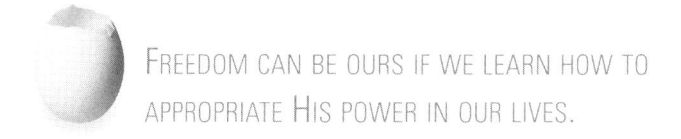

> FREEDOM CAN BE OURS IF WE LEARN HOW TO APPROPRIATE HIS POWER IN OUR LIVES.

life, and we are not without power. All of these things have been put under the feet of Jesus, which means that freedom can be ours if we learn how to appropriate His power in our lives.

TRANSFORMING POWER

How do we access and appropriate the power of the Holy Spirit? How does it work through us? How does it change us? Remember, we find our true reflection in the Word of God, and the Word transforms us by its power. The process of transformation begins with this verse: "I beseech you therefore, brethren, by the mercies of God, that ye present your bodies a living sacrifice, holy, acceptable unto God, which is your reasonable service. And be not conformed to this world: but be ye transformed by the renewing of your mind, that ye may prove what is that good, and acceptable, and perfect, will of God" (Romans 12:1-2).

You are going to have to give God ownership of your physical body if you want to live in victory. You have to let Him take over. The result is that you will be able to prove, or "manifest," those things that are good, acceptable, and the perfect will of God. Notice how this reverses the entire process of destruction that has been initiated by the spirit of darkness. Instead of manifesting death and destruction in your flesh, you will manifest goodness and the perfect will of God!

There is no limit to the power of the Holy Spirit to change your physical condition. Note the word "changed" in 2 Corinthians 3:18: "But we all, with open face beholding as in a glass the glory of the Lord, are ***changed*** into the same image from glory to glory, even as by the Spirit of the Lord." The word t*ransformed* is translated from the same Greek word, *metamorphoo,* which literally means to form a change of condition. This is not some theoretical, emotional, or surreal response. It is an actual physiological change.

Do you realize that when you are either raptured or raised from the dead, you will be given a new glorified body that signifies the final stage of your transformation? You will be able to walk through walls. Hallelujah! There will be no restrictions, limitations, sickness, or struggles in your glorified body. The only thing that is keeping us from manifesting that now is the corruption that is still present in the outer man. But that doesn't mean that we should be content with suffering and destruction while we are living this life.

Romans 8:11 says, "But if the Spirit of him that raised up Jesus from the dead dwell in you, he that raised up Christ from the dead shall also quicken your mortal bodies by his Spirit that dwelleth in you." He will quicken, or make alive, our ***mortal*** bodies. This will happen to your body, which is still subject to death; the one you are sitting in right now. The Holy Spirit who dwells in you is going to make your body alive ***now***. You see, this power purge is something that happens because of who you are in Christ, but the power really comes from the Spirit of God. It is the hand of the Lord in you—His Spirit working through your spirit and changing you.

As you begin to act upon the Word of God that is sown into your spirit, you go into the transformation process. How long does it last? As long as you are living in this earth. You are continually in a state of being transformed until the final enemy—physical death—is defeated. Your victory over physical death will take place in the resurrection. In other words, there is nothing in your life, short of physical death, that cannot be overcome by the transforming power of God. All of the enemies of Christ are beneath our feet.

YIELD…THEN RULE AND REIGN

The next step is found in Romans 6:12-14 which says, "Let not sin therefore reign in your mortal body, that ye should obey it in the lusts thereof. Neither yield ye your members as instruments of unrighteousness unto sin: but yield yourselves unto God, as those that are alive from the dead, and your members as instruments of righteousness unto God. For sin shall not have dominion over you: for ye are not under the law, but under grace."

Now, who do you think these instructions are meant for? They are not meant for your physical man; they are addressing the ***real*** you—your inner man. God is saying, "Stand up on the inside and take dominion over your body that is still subject to death. Don't let sin take over—don't let the enemy use and abuse you any longer. Yield yourself to Me and rule and reign

> HOW DO YOU YIELD YOURSELF TO GOD?
> YOU HAVE TO DO THE WORKS OF GOD.
> YOU HAVE TO LET HIM USE YOU.

over yourself with My power working through you." How do you yield yourself to God? You have to do the works of God. You have to let Him use you. You have to surrender control of your life to Him. If you choose not to do that, you have effectively cut off the power.

Now, many people cringe at the idea of being "used." There are so many wounded Christians who have been victimized by abuse or, at the very least, have had their trust violated in such a way that they are afraid to relinquish control and submit themselves to someone else. Sadly, this is a very common occurrence in the church today. But there is nothing to fear about surrendering to God—He is righteous and just, and He loves you without restraint. You can trust Him completely.

Being used is a good thing—as long as it is God who is using you. It's a wonderful experience to be used of God. And if you allow Him to use you, He can transform you. If you will not be used, if you cannot surrender to Him, then you can't change. You'll stay locked in carnality and bound by the spirit of darkness. Until believers allow God to use their members, or their bodies, they are not going to change. The power of the Holy Spirit has to come through your members to purge you. Just like darkness coming through your members produces sin, the power of God working through your members purges and changes you.

RESURRECTION POWER

The final key to the power purge is found in 1 Corinthians 15:

> *Listen, I tell you a mystery: We will not all sleep, but we will all be changed—in a flash, in the twinkling of an eye, at the last trumpet. For the trumpet will sound, the dead will be raised imperishable, and we will be changed. For the perishable must clothe itself with the imperishable, and the mortal with immortality. When the perishable has been clothed with the imperishable, and the mortal with immortality, then the saying that is written will come true: "Death has been swallowed up in victory."*
>
> —1 Corinthians 15:51-54 NIV

When the apostle Paul wrote these words to the church of Corinth, he was anticipating a final victory over death. "We will not all sleep," means that we will not all experience a physical death. Obviously, Paul died a natural death, but his victory will come at the resurrection, and those believers who are still living when the trumpet sounds and Christ appears will not taste death.

Every indication in Scripture seems to tell us that we are in those days. Whether the Lord returns in two years or twenty, there are likely those among us who will experience that miraculous event. But that does not in any way minimize the truth of this passage that applies to all of us—and that is that while some of us will not taste death, ***all of us will be changed***. Paul is speaking about the same power mentioned in Romans 8:11—the power that raised Jesus from the dead will make alive your mortal body. Paul is saying that you will have this life-changing, transforming power this side of the resurrection—in this life, and in this body. The power that purges out every remnant of spiritual darkness.

SURRENDER ALL

Perhaps you are familiar with the old hymn that says, "I surrender all. I surrender all. All to Jesus, I surrender. I surrender all." Many times people have used that as a point of declaration for their salvation—but the reality is that surrendering is an ongoing process. It is a life-long commitment that goes beyond simple acceptance of Jesus Christ as Savior to making Him Lord over every aspect of our lives.

> HE IS WORTHY OF YOUR TRUST. HE DOESN'T WANT TO RUIN YOUR LIFE—HE WANTS TO GIVE YOU HOPE AND A FUTURE.

Whatever the Lord wants to use you for, and however He wants to do it, is something that is between Him and you. What I do know is that His plan is a wonderful one: "'For I know the plans I have for you,' declares the LORD, 'plans to prosper you and not to harm you, plans to give you hope and a future'" (Jeremiah 29:11). He is worthy of your trust. He doesn't want to ruin your life—He wants to give you hope and a future.

He isn't asking that you surrender to any other individual. Jesus is the one who died for you. He shed His precious blood for your sins. He is jealous over you and will not let you be controlled by another person. Churches, pastors, and other leaders in the body of Christ can help facilitate His plan, and can present opportunities for you to serve God, but if you submit yourself to Him, He is the One who is going to use you. You are ultimately accountable to Him, not to other people.

Practically speaking, how do we surrender ourselves to God? It begins with your relationship with the Lord. If you are surrendered to Him, then you are going to have a committed devotional life. It means that you have a close, intimate relationship with Him. You walk and talk with Him; He is with you, and you are with Him every day. You know Him and as a result, you know His voice. When He calls you to acts of obedience, you'll know what those things are because you know Him.

Then you have to lay your life down on the altar. One of the first things many Christians have to relinquish is their own ambitions, dreams, and plans. For instance, you might think that your career is of God, but in reality, if you haven't yielded control of that area of your life, then your career *is* your god. You see, if you have totally surrendered that part of your life to God, it doesn't make any difference to you what you do for a living. Whatever He wants is enough motivation, and you are happy and content to obey Him and work as unto Him.

Others think that if they are striving to take care of their financial obligations and support their families, then they must be pleasing God. But that isn't the same thing as being surrendered either, because for some people, their family is their god. He wants us to care for our families and be responsible—but more than that He wants us to be obedient to Him, and not make our loved ones a higher priority than our commitment to Him.

The same thing applies to the church—there are plenty of Christians out there who are serving the church rather than serving God first. They place their trust in the establishment of the church, rather than surrendering to the head of the church, who is Jesus. This is why so many people who don't even know Jesus are "serving" in our churches. Going to church regularly is not the same as being surrendered to God—He isn't impressed by works.

Every single believer has been called of God to surrender himself—spirit, soul, and body. Ultimately, surrender is God working through you. And if you are doing what He tells you to do, it will be works of righteousness. Your career will glorify Him and bear fruit for the kingdom. Your family will be provided for, and you will walk in blessing and abundance. You will delight in being faithful to serve the local church in which He has placed you. You will minister to people, share the good news of Christ, pray for the sick, and serve the Lord in everything that you do.

> He can't work His life-changing power in your life until you hand over control in every area, holding nothing back.

Have you fully surrendered yourself to God? If not, it is critical that you not put it off any longer. He can't work His life-changing power in your life until you hand over control in every area, holding nothing back. If you are ready to allow the Holy Spirit free reign in your life, then pray the following prayer from your heart:

Heavenly Father, without You I am nothing. Lord Jesus, in You I am the righteousness of God, but if I don't yield myself to You I stay bound. Today, I make a decision to surrender to You. I turn my life completely over to You. I lay my body as a living sacrifice upon the altar of Your service.

Lord Jesus, I want a deep relationship with You. I want to know You, and I want to know Your voice. I want to know Your will for my life, and I want to serve You with gladness. Lord Jesus, You and I have big things to do in this earth, and I want to do my part. So I surrender myself—everything that I am, everything that I have, everything I have ever hoped for. And I do it joyfully, trusting You to complete every good work that You have started in my life.

Thank You, Holy Spirit, for your awesome power that purges out all opposition in my outer man. My flesh will bow its knee as I do what You tell me to do. Thank You, Jesus, for my total freedom. Thank You for my new life in You. I give You all glory and honor. In the name of Jesus. Amen.

Study Guide

Since mankind's fall in the Garden of Eden, a chasm of separation has existed between man and God. But Jesus Christ bridged the gap and made it possible for you to walk in communion with God once again. How could you not want to remove every remnant of your old, sinful nature? Allow the Holy Spirit to purge everything that is not of Him, and you will be able to appropriate His power, victory, and blessings in your life. Allow the Word to transform you by its power, and you will be able to walk in an intimate, loving relationship with God.

1. How has the fallen nature of man affected the earth and physical lives of people living today? What solution is there for the problems perpetuated by the curse and mankind's sinful state? How do you access and appropriate the power of the Holy Spirit? How does it work through you?

2. God has called you to rule and reign. How does yielding yourself to God actually give you dominion in the Earth? What is the true position of your new inner man in Christ? Why is it so important that you allow God to use you?

About the Author

Randy Gilbert, along with his wife and co-pastor Cherie, founded Faith Landmarks Ministries in Richmond, Virginia in 1980. They are also founders of Faith Landmarks Bible Institute and Faith Landmarks Ministries World Outreach Center. They pastor a growing congregation of more than 7,000 people that carries a strong emphasis on helps and equipping the saints to do the work of the ministry.

Other Books by Randy Gilbert

Bought by Babylon
Victory over Depression
The Power Push
God's Program Is the Local Church
What Jesus Did for You At Calvary
From Heaven to Earth—The Real Meaning of Christmas
Faith with an Attitude
Seasons In Christ Devotional

If you have enjoyed this book, or it has blessed your life, we would like to hear from you. Please contact us at:

Faith Landmarks Ministries
8491 Chamberlayne Road
Richmond, VA 23227
(804) 262-7104

Visit our Web site at:
www.contact.tv